Published by Christian Art Publishers
PO Box 1599, Vereeniging, 1930, RSA

© 2022
First edition 2022

Designed by Christian Art Publishers
Devotions taken from *Hold on to Hope* by Jimi le Roux

Cover designed by Christian Art Publishers
Images used under license from Shutterstock.com

Scripture quotations are taken from the Holy Bible,
English Standard Version®. ESV® Text Edition: 2016.
Copyright © 2001 by Crossway, a publishing ministry of
Good News Publishers. Used by permission. All rights reserved.

Scripture quotations marked NLT are taken from the Holy Bible,
New Living Translation, copyright © 1996, 2004, 2015
by Tyndale House Foundation. Used by permission of
Tyndale House Publishers, Carol Stream, Illinois 60188.
All rights reserved.

Scripture quotations marked KJV are taken from the Holy Bible,
King James Version, and are in the public domain.

Scripture quotations marked NKJV are taken from
the New King James Version®. Copyright © 1979, 1980, 1982
by Thomas Nelson, Inc. Used by permission. All rights reserved.

Scripture quotations marked CEV are from the
Contemporary English Version. Copyright © 1991, 1992, 1995
by American Bible Society. Used by permission.

Scripture quotations marked MSG are taken from The Message,
copyright © 1993, 1994, 1995, 1996, 2000, 2001, 2002 by
Eugene H. Peterson. Used by permission of NavPress.
All rights reserved.

Printed in China

ISBN 978-1-77637-173-0

© All rights reserved. No part of this book may be reproduced in any
form without permission in writing from the publisher, except in the
case of brief quotations in critical articles or reviews.

22 23 24 25 26 27 28 29 30 31 – 10 9 8 7 6 5 4 3 2 1

MINI DEVOTIONS

FOR
TODAY

1
The way to blessing

> Blessed is the man who walks not in the
> counsel of the wicked, nor stands in the way
> of sinners, nor sits in the seat of scoffers.
>
> PSALM 1:111

The purpose of the book of Psalms is indeed to show the way to a blessed life. Such a life is always a life with God, a life in relationship with Him. Blessings cannot be had apart from God, because it is He who blesses!

This psalm says we cannot allow anyone or anything to detract us from living a life with God. If we "walk" among those who do not know God, we may later "stand," that is become comfortable, with those who do wrong. After all, "everyone does it". No, that must never happen!

It is true that believers have unbelieving friends, and that is good and necessary. But our friends should see our faith, be drawn to God, and be changed. Then they, too, will be blessed!

God who blesses, I want to live in Your blessing.
Let my walking, standing, and sitting glorify You! Amen.

2

Abide in the Word

*He is like a tree planted by streams of water
that yields its fruit in its season, and its leaf does
not wither. In all that he does, he prospers.*

PSALM 1:3

If you abide in the Word and the Word abides in you, you will develop depth, maturity, wisdom. You will become stronger as your knowledge of God increases. Your fullness of the Spirit – of which the water here is a symbol – will become apparent in your fruit: love, joy, peace, patience, goodness, faithfulness, etc. (Gal. 5:22-23).

People will want to be near you because they will recognize your faith. You will prosper in all that you do. Take note that prosperity in the Bible is not just about material wealth – it is about having God with you.

Living with God means to draw from His strength and peace. It means that you can handle anything! Having God with you is shalom – the result of a deep relationship with Him.

*Lord, let me abide in You, as You abide in me;
and let me bear fruit to Your glory. Amen.*

3

My shield and my glory

But You, O Lord, are a shield about me,
my glory, and the lifter of my head.

PSALM 3:3

David wrote these words as he was fleeing from Absalom, who staged a coup against his throne. It was David's own doing, as his sin with Bathsheba was now catching up with him. David was acutely aware of his shame, but had pleaded for mercy and forgiveness. And now, while being chased, he simply clung to God, because he had nowhere else to go. He radically believed that God would remain with him because of their covenant. So he just trusted and waited for God to save him and restore his honor.

Let's stay on the straight and the narrow – yes, by all means possible. Still, we stray, and sometimes we stray far. The lesson here, however, is that God does not stray away. God remains true, even when we are untrue. That's His character.

Lift your head, therefore. God is still here; God is still involved!

Lord, save me from myself.
Restore me when I fall. Amen.

4

Morning prayer

> I lay down and slept; I woke again,
> for the Lord sustained me.
>
> PSALM 3:5

David woke up with the realization that he had slept well. Remember that he was a fugitive at this stage with his pursuers hot on his heels – not exactly cause for a good night's rest! Still, in the next verse he maintains that he will not be afraid of even ten thousand enemies around him. He has the peace of the Lord!

Nowadays, our stress is more psychological. Worry, failure, and relationship problems create tension in our bodies that prevent us from relaxing and rejuvenating rest. It does help to be physically active during the day (especially in natural sunlight) and to keep good sleep habits: avoiding coffee and electronic devices, and turning the lights low.

However, David's peace came from God. He felt secure, because his Covenant God was with him. Why wouldn't he sleep well – he had radical faith!

> You, O Lord, are my shield and strength.
> Teach me to trust You and to then relax. Amen.

5
More joy

You have put more joy in my heart than
they have when their grain and wine abound.

PSALM 4:7

These words by David refer specifically to people who have just harvested, whose barns are filled with grain, grapes, and fruit. Harvest time is a joyful time in all agrarian communities, and harvest festivals are always filled with exuberance and abundance.

David felt, however, that he had even more joy than this. Of course we can rejoice over a plentiful harvest, a solid return, an unexpected bonus, or a time of financial security. Why shouldn't we? We should really be able to enjoy life and celebrate it with vigor! Still, like David, we also know that there is more to life. There is a deeper joy.

What David felt with God surpassed all the festivals he ever attended! The fact is that we can long for more in the middle of the biggest celebration, or just be happy in God with relatively few earthly things, as long as He is in the picture – that's what's important!

*Lord, You are my joy. To live
with You is a celebration! Amen.*

6
Daybreak with God

O Lord, in the morning You hear my voice; in the
morning I prepare a sacrifice for You and watch.

PSALM 5:3

How wonderful the mornings are! Before electricity, when people were still synchronized to the sun's rhythm, they went to sleep when it became dark and got up at dawn. The people of old saw the sun come up every morning, while today we scarcely ever see that majestic natural miracle.

Mornings, however, are the best part of the day: the air is fresh and cool, the colors are deep and bright, and the birds chirp about. Our first coffee should be had outside! Mornings are also ideal for spending time with God – reading, praying, and pondering. It's the most popular quiet time for a reason.

David spent time with God in the morning, and Jesus got up early to pray. So did almost all of the saints of the past and present. Let's rediscover mornings – and make God part of the picture!

Lord, I want to meet You in the morning! Amen.

7
My shield is God

My shield is with God, who saves the upright in heart.

PSALM 7:10

David complains about the unrighteousness around him – there is just too much godlessness, injustice, and violence! He pleads for God to intervene and set things right.

We have the same need, don't we? David finds consolation, though, in the fact that God is his "shield" – a common symbol in Scripture for protection or safety. For David, it is a given that God defends the "upright." What does uprightness mean, though? Uprightness alludes to doing right, but the essence is a heart that is right: authentic and sincere, without masks or facades.

It is what it is – you get what you see! Mistakes are not hidden away, but taken responsibility for. With such a person, as David indeed was, God can do much. However, with insincerity and artificiality one doesn't get far. Get under God's shield with the right attitude!

Lord, make me upright and be my shield! Amen.

8

Sadness and glory

> Yet You have made him a little lower than the heavenly
> beings and crowned him with glory and honor.
>
> PSALM 8:5

David is in awe about the majesty of creation and even asks: "What is man that you are mindful of him?" (Ps. 8:4).

Our natural answer would be that man is completely insignificant, a mere speck in the greatness of the universe. But that is wrong! David correctly puts man right on top of creation – just below God and the angels. Man has been placed above the whole created world, because he is the image of God, the crown of creation. He was created to rule over it all! That is man's purpose.

Therefore, whenever we see a destitute or broken person, it is a far cry from the honor that God bestowed on man. It is the tragic result of sin.

It should make us exceedingly sad! God's will is that everyone should be restored to dignity and worth, that his or her crown should be returned.

*Lord, it is sad to see so many people
dishonored and fallen. Help me; help us! Amen.*

9
God chooses

> He has established His throne for justice,
> and He judges the world with righteousness;
> He judges the peoples with uprightness.
>
> PSALM 9:7-8

One of the best-known images of God is that of a judge. We often read in the Bible, as in this verse, that God is a "righteous" judge. We know that He also demands "righteousness" of us.

Righteousness means "to be right," and it has two sides. First, we need to be right with God, meaning that we only do what He expects. Then, we need to be right with others, meaning that we act with fairness and consideration. Be one of the "righteous" that the Bible speaks of! Remember that God stands for what is right, and that He stands on the side of what is right – never on the side of what is wrong.

If your case is right, God will be on your side. With such a case, you can proceed. Never find yourself on the side of wrongdoing – you won't find God there!

Lord, let me act in justness and fairness.
Also, let me add grace to justice, as You have done! Amen.

10

God won't forget

> For the needy shall not always be forgotten,
> and the hope of the poor shall not perish forever.
> PSALM 9:18

Sometimes people think God has forgotten them, but God cannot and will not forget. He is especially concerned for the needy and the afflicted, the humble and the lowly. God is especially on the side of those who depend on Him.

Why then, if we are needy, do we sometimes have to wait so long for His answer? Think of faith as sowing a seed. When you sow a field, it doesn't mean that there will be an instant harvest. The sowed field might look to you as if nothing is happening, but that's not true. The seed is there, under the ground, growing. Such a field has all the potential for a harvest, while an unsowed field has none!

God did not forget you! He is busy with you, but perhaps He intends more for you than you expected. Keep sowing in faith, for your harvest will come!

*Lord, help me to faithfully keep on trusting.
I will wait for Your time to come. Amen.*

11

No more fear

You defend orphans and everyone else in need, so
that no one on earth can terrify others again.

PSALM 10:18 (CEV)

God is a reality and where God is, terror and fear are dispelled. It is a well-known biblical fact that God wants to take our fears away. Still, we struggle to let go of fear.

We must remember that fear is the body's primary mechanism for keeping us safe. When we are afraid, we are extremely conscious of danger and can avoid it. There are circumstances, though, in which fear becomes a habit. Fear can also become misplaced or expressed in inappropriate or damaging ways. How do we live wisely with fear? Of course, we need to take reasonable precautions against danger. After that, though, fear has no useful function. Then it becomes counter-productive and destructive.

Fear often then becomes the danger, and we become our own enemy! Confess the following: God is in control of what happens. God keeps me safe. God frees me from fear. Repeat it as necessary – it is the truth!

Lord, I will no longer fear; I will trust in You. Amen.

12

Silver words

> The words of the LORD are pure words, like silver refined
> in a furnace on the ground, purified seven times.
>
> PSALM 12:6

In this psalm, David is speaking out about the corrupt and deceitful words of the godless. Opposed to that, he defines God's words as "silver, purified seven times." A beautiful image, isn't it?

God's words are pure, costly, the truth – worthy of seeking and finding! There is also a lesson for us in this. Our own words should likewise be "pure," even before we say them. The Word says that to speak without control is foolish. It also says that we should be quick to listen but slow to speak. Yes, let's post a guard before that mouth of ours! Let's think before we speak. A good start is just to say less.

Above all, let's be guided by the Holy Spirit, because self-control is His fruit. Allow the Spirit to filter out all falseness, self-centeredness, and harshness from our words. Then our speech will be gracious, pleasant, and powerful as well!

Holy Spirit, purify my heart.
Then my words will be pure too. Amen.

13

On my side!

God is on the side of every good person. You may
spoil the plans of the poor, but the LORD protects them.

PSALM 14:5-6 (CEV)

It's wonderful how simple David's worldview was – typical of those times. He says God is on the side of the righteous and that is it! Let's just accept this wonderful truth.

Yes, simply take it as your personal truth. Write "God is on my side" in your journal, or put it on your notice board. David says this fact is true for anyone who is righteous, here translated as a "good person." Is a righteous person someone without sin or mistakes? Oh no, it is someone who knows his sin all too well and flees to God for His help. It is someone who is deeply dependent on God, who has made Him his refuge!

Such a one has been made righteous by God because of Christ. Go get your righteousness from Him and then remember, God is completely on YOUR SIDE. He is!

Thank You, Lord, for being so completely FOR ME. Amen.

14
My all is You

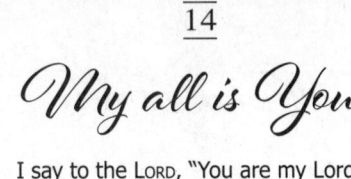

> I say to the LORD, "You are my Lord;
> I have no good apart from You."
>
> PSALM 16:2

David says to the "Lord" (his Covenant God, *Yahweh*) that He is his "Lord" (*Adonai*), in other words his master, his boss. God is the Master of his life. A beautiful confession!

Still, David takes it deeper. He not only submits to his Master, but absolutely rejoices in his submission. In fact, David declares that God is the only good he possesses. He means that nothing of the many good things that he had – being king of Israel – came close to experiencing God.

God is the only real source of David's joy and fulfillment. No wonder David was a man after God's heart! God can also be first in our lives – the first source of our joy, the meaning of our lives, and the best we can hope for. Where He is the Master, we have joy and peace and meaning and hope. He makes everything good. See it like David did!

God, You bring goodness to my life.
You bring me joy and purpose! Amen.

15

It's beautiful!

> The LORD is my chosen portion and my cup;
> You hold my lot. The lines have fallen for me in
> pleasant places; indeed, I have a beautiful inheritance.
>
> PSALM 16:5-6

In this psalm David is full of joy and gratitude. He looks around him and feels absolutely blessed. He says, "What I have received, comes all from God." Everything that God has measured out to him is beautiful. Remember, this psalm is not about the fact that David was a king and had many treasures.

No, it's about David's heart and relationship with God. Other kings might reason that they still have too little or believe that they have obtained all their possessions by their own effort. David, on the other hand, gives the glory to God. We, too, can look around us and decide that our portion is too little or too inferior.

Remember, some people feel thankful and blessed with little while others are unsatisfied and angry amidst plenty. That's our choice – to feel blessed or not. Yes, indeed! Choose gratitude and contentment, choose blessing!

Lord, help me to look around
and see Your blessings. Amen.

16

I love you

> I love You, O LORD, my strength. The LORD is my
> rock and my fortress and my deliverer, my God,
> my rock, in whom I take refuge, my shield,
> and the horn of my salvation, my stronghold.
>
> PSALM 18:1-2

What is the Great Commandment? The Great Commandment is that you shall love your God – with your whole heart, soul, and mind, and all your strength (Mark 12:30).

So, do you love God? In this context do not try to feel love for God as a warm and fuzzy feeling. Rather, start by confessing that you do love God. Say it to Him as David did: "I love You, O Lord!" Declaring your love is your conversion and submission, your transformation, your sanctification! By confessing it, you will grow in it.

See how beautifully David then motivates his declaration of love. God is his fortress, his shield, his salvation, his stronghold. You can also tell God why you love Him. You know, that is what worship is!

Loving Father, I do love You!
Teach me what it means. Amen.

17

You get what you give

> With the merciful You show Yourself merciful;
> with the blameless man You show Yourself blameless;
> with the purified You show Yourself pure; and with
> the crooked You make Yourself seem tortuous.
>
> PSALM 18:25-26

There is a wonderful reciprocal principle in the Bible that we reap what we sow. Those who give love will receive love, those who forgive will be forgiven, and the ones who bless become the blessed ones.

Here we read it again: the merciful will find mercy; the faithful will find faithfulness. With the measure you use it will be measured to you, Jesus declared (Matt. 7:2). Even if we give a disciple a cup of cold water because of Christ, we will receive the reward of a disciple. The opposite, however, is also true – as we judge we will be judged, and as we condemn we will be condemned.

As you are, you perceive your world. I pray that your heart will be simple and pure, loving and kind! Then that will be the life you have.

> Holy Lord, make me pure, kind,
> and true. Make me like You! Amen.

18

Who else is a rock?

For who is God, but the Lord?
And who is a rock, except our God?
PSALM 18:31

To describe God as a rock is a well-known metaphor in the Bible. We already see it, for example, in Moses' song at the end of Deuteronomy. What does the image mean?

Well, a rock always stands for solidity and security, because a rock is immovable. On a rock you can build your home, you can anchor your life. That is how God is! If the winds and storms come – for they will come – we will not perish, because He is stronger than any storm. It is interesting to often read in Scripture that the Rock is the only rock. There is just no other God onto whom you can anchor your life.

You could just as well anchor yourself to your own boat – it would mean nothing! No, there is only one Rock, and that is *Elohim*, our God. Whatever is not built on Him will surely perish.

Lord, You are the fixed point in this chaos
around me, my anchor in this storm. Amen.

19

The day testifies

> The heavens declare the glory of God, and the sky above proclaims His handiwork. Day to day pours out speech, and night to night reveals knowledge.
>
> PSALM 19:1-2

David says that nature constantly declares God's goodness and glory. He poetically describes how one day pours its report of God's greatness into the next – from the first creation day right until this morning! When the sun rises in its grandeur, it testifies about God's shining glory.

When dusk sets in and the moon shines bright and clear, it affirms that God was trustworthy once again. Think of the rolling planets and the immeasurable stars, the powerful forces that hold atoms together and the ever-expanding universe. All of this testifies about God's fantastic power and might. Stand in awe thereof – see God in it! Then, pass the testimony on. Let people see your faith, hope, and love – it honors Him!

Then tell someone about God's goodness. Let them know about something God did. Encourage others to trust the good God you know!

Yes, wonderful God, I do want to be
a witness of Your goodness and grace! Amen.

20

Desirable, costly, rich

> More to be desired are they than gold,
> even much fine gold; sweeter also than
> honey and drippings of the honeycomb.
>
> PSALM 19:10

This psalm starts off with nature as God's general revelation, but then it turns to His Word as His special revelation. David says, for example, that God's Word – referring to the Law – is perfect and trustworthy. It brings healing and shows the right path.

See God's Word from a modern perspective: What would computer equipment be without a program? Merely unusable metal and plastic. It needs a program, software. Similarly, God's Word supplies the program on which we live – the software that guides our behavior and life. Remove it, and we wouldn't know what to do. Program it in, and our life has meaning, direction, and purpose.

It supplies the facts of where you come from, what you're here for, and where you're supposed to go. Program the Word daily into your soul, and experience its direction and purpose for yourself!

*Lord, Your Word is indeed dear to me –
like gold, like honey! It gives meaning to my life. Amen.*

21

The God of your fathers

> May the LORD answer you in the day of trouble!
> May the name of the God of Jacob protect you!
>
> PSALM 20:1

In this psalm David asks that God will hear and protect the king – just as He did for Jacob, their forefather. Jacob experienced God intensely in his lifelong struggle to obtain the covenant promise. David, who is the king at this stage, wants to live his life in the same way.

Do you have a similar desire? Did you have a father or mother who truly served God – or a grandmother, or some other mentor or role model? You cannot relive their relationship with God, but you can have your own. You can write your own story-with-God with the same passion, trust, and commitment that they had.

You can have God in your life, see Him working, hear His voice, and experience His guidance. Then your own children will want to follow the God of their father or mother, too!

Yes, Lord, I do want to show my children how to live with God. God of my fathers, help me! Amen.

22

Words with power

> May He grant you your heart's
> desire and fulfill all your plans!
>
> PSALM 20:4

What a beautiful blessing the Word pronounces here – over me and you! Remember, a blessing in Jesus' name, spoken in faith and accepted in faith, is a powerful confirmation of God's goodness and intention. It changes lives! Just think of the effect that it had on you when an adult or a teacher acknowledged your worth as a youngster, perhaps pointing out your strengths or assuring you of your future success.

It was very encouraging! We remember such affirmations forever. It's the same when we declare God's blessing over someone: "God loves you; God cares for you; God will fulfill your desires." Such pronouncements are empowering and faith building. Make sure to bless others with such words! Please, please avoid telling a child the opposite: that he will fail or that she is not good enough. It robs them of their very life; it binds them inwardly – and it's not true at all!

No, Jesus said to bless, never curse (Matt. 5:44).

Loving Father, make all my words a blessing! Amen.

23
Hoist His banner!

May we shout for joy over your salvation,
and in the name of our God set up our banners!
May the Lord fulfill all your petitions!

PSALM 20:5

David is referring to the battles of Israel, but we also battle, don't we? Take note that David's battles are fought "in the name of our God" and that the victory is also God's. Therein we find our key.

Our struggles are most often only our private little struggles – often about a bruised ego. As we grow spiritually, however, we will learn that our ego is not the center of our lives. On the contrary, we learn to "crucify" our ego and to focus on God and His will for us. We also learn to just leave some battles for Him to fight.

Let us ultimately learn, though, to fight His battles, to fight His enemies, to advance His interests, and to let His kingdom come.

When we fight this way, victory is assured!

> Lord, fight for me as You have promised –
> and let me also fight for Your sake! Amen.

24

Praise God

> Yet You are holy, enthroned on the praises of Israel.
>
> PSALM 22:3

This verse can be understood to mean that God "indwells" the praises of His people. We really experience it as such: when we start praising God, we sense His presence more and more.

Especially in our crises, when we so need God's presence, our praise-in-faith soon brings peace and victory.

Like Paul and Silas who sang to God's glory in prison in the middle of the night, we can also experience God, even in our darkest hours. However, let's not think that mere words of praise can bring God near. It does not work mechanically! No, true praise is focusing our hearts on God, turning to Him who is already present anyway. Praise is becoming more and more aware of His presence!

Words that do not mirror the praise of our hearts will remain only words – they are not praise as such. However, if our hearts burn for Him even in our difficulty, we will experience His faith, His victory, His presence!

Lord, help me to win over the darkness
by focusing on the light. Amen.

25

Here is my God

He trusts in the LORD; let Him deliver him;
let Him rescue him, for he delights in Him!

PSALM 22:8

David's thoughts are dark, because things are not going well at all. He is mocked and despised. He feels unworthy and humiliated. It is a bitter thought for him that God can intervene but doesn't.

This causes his enemies to ask, "Where is your God now?" David is wondering the same! He pleads for God to prove Himself to the whole world, yet experiences the opposite. We can identify with David here. We also live as believers in an unbelieving world. We sometimes feel excluded or rejected, even ridiculed. It is especially bad when others make snide remarks about faith, believers, or God. Remember, that's part of our Christian life!

We so want God to prove Himself to the world, but it doesn't work that way. However, you can help people see God in your words and actions, in your life! Do that as well as you can – the Spirit will help you.

*Lord, make me a living testimony
of Your goodness and power. Amen.*

26

God is there

> Save me from the mouth of the lion! You have
> rescued me from the horns of the wild oxen!
>
> PSALM 22:21

Even in David's darkest thoughts there remains an undercurrent of faith, because he is sharing his dark thoughts with God. He still believes! Perhaps it was this talking-it-through-with-God that built his faith, because now, at the lowest point, his spirit lights up.

He now realizes that his deliverance is assured – he must only persevere; he must just see it through! Soon it will all be over. You and I can experience a crisis in two ways. If we are *without hope*, it can really feel as if God is gone and that everything is lost. We are fixed on the worst-case scenario. Then the realization can dawn, though, that God is still present, that He is still in control. That changes everything!

Suddenly we have hope – and biblical hope is a very powerful thing – and our strength returns. Oh, pray that your hope and strength reignites, because the fact is this: God is near!

*Lord, switch on hope in my heart –
renew my strength! Amen.*

27

Everything for today

You, Lord, are my shepherd. I will never be in need.

PSALM 23:1 (CEV)

Now to the well-known, best-loved and most beautiful psalm! Matter-of-factly, in simple and straightforward terms, David spells out the result of God being our shepherd: "I will never be in need." The King James Version reads, "I shall not want."

This tremendously powerful statement contains one of the keys to our walk with God, a key that can unlock the whole spiritual life. Please accept it as the absolute truth: with God you have what you need – every day! He gives you enough for the day.

With God present, you have sufficient resources to handle every situation. Today you will have enough to do today's tasks, to surmount today's challenges. God is enough for you today. Tomorrow will be the same.

If we can accept in faith that God really is a Good Shepherd who will give us what we need for today, we can have peace. That is what total surrender means.

*Good Shepherd, I trust You. You will supply
what I really need in this situation. Amen.*

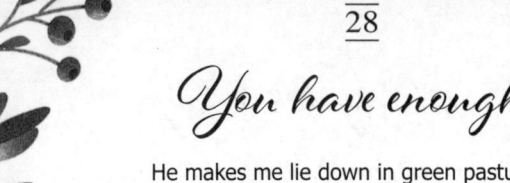

You have enough

He makes me lie down in green pastures.
He leads me beside still waters.

PSALM 23:2

The shepherd must make sure that his sheep always have sufficient grazing and ample water. In order for that to happen, the shepherd had to move his flock around. Sometimes they had to go far and stay away for months. The shepherd knew where good grazing was available and where the water holes were.

It is the same way with the Good Shepherd's sheep. These verses do not imply that we will always, leisurely, remain at green pastures and still waters. No, life has its seasons, and sometimes we will trek, hot and thirsty, through areas in which we find little comfort. Still, we will always end up, as often as necessary, with sufficient provision for our needs, with rest, and with comfort.

That is the task of the Good Shepherd. Trust Him for that! You can have this peace: "I shall not want" (Ps. 23:1). Yes, your needs will be met.

Good Shepherd, thank You that You will lead me to
green pastures again, to still waters. Amen.

29

Welcome to the feast!

> You treat me to a feast, while my
> enemies watch. You honor me as Your guest,
> and You fill my cup until it overflows.
> PSALM 23:5 (CEV)

Psalm 23 consists of three parts: life, death, and eternity. It is first about green pastures and still waters, rest for the soul and the paths of righteousness. This is all about life's abundance and God's blessing. Then we get to the "valley of the shadow of death," through which all of us must pass, but God is also there!

Then the whole tone of the psalm changes – it becomes a jubilation! God receives me as His guest at the heavenly feast. Yes, when all is over and done, when you have given *all* to finish the race, God is waiting for you at the winning post! Then you will be received as a hero and your victory celebrated!

Then your struggle and worry, your pain will be taken away, and you will enter rest. Be encouraged: that day is coming!

> Lord, I praise You for the gift of life –
> and for the gift of eternal life. Amen.

30

Goodness and mercy

Surely goodness and mercy shall follow me all the days of
my life, and I shall dwell in the house of the Lord forever.

PSALM 23:6

David makes the powerful pronouncement that "goodness and mercy" will follow him all the days of his life. What a statement of faith!

Make it your own. Write it down and repeat it to yourself so that it sinks down into your soul and changes your identity. You are a beloved of God! Goodness and mercy is your inheritance! If you have trouble, it is temporary. David then adds that he will "dwell in the house of the Lord forever." He means that he will remain near God's temple for the rest of his life. But we have a far greater expectation. The temple of God is in our hearts and it will endure forever!

Take note: the goodness and mercy that we experience in this life can never compare to the goodness and mercy and love and peace and joy of eternal life with God!

*Father, thank You that the door to
Your house is always, always open to me! Amen.*

31

God's way

> Make me to know Your ways, O LORD;
> teach me Your paths. Lead me in Your truth
> and teach me, for You are the God of
> my salvation; for You I wait all the day long.
> PSALM 25:4-5

In his distress, David urgently asks for God's intervention! He is very anxious, but then he comes up with something rather mature. He not only asks for deliverance out of the situation, he asks for God's will in the situation.

This is important, because we often think prayer is basically to write our will onto God's agenda. But we forget that God might have His own intention in the process – we mostly assume that God's will in a matter is exactly the same as our will! David, however, asks for God's will and paths so that his will can align with God's will more closely.

Yes, perhaps we should stop asking God for what we want and start listening for what God wants. Let's speak less and listen more, because God is God.

> Lord, what is Your will for me today?
> What will honor You now? Amen.

32

A spiritual test

Prove me, O Lord, and try me; test my heart and my mind.
PSALM 26:2

David opens up his heart toward God and asks Him to examine his motives and thoughts, his words and deeds, and to show him whatever there may be that does not please Him.

He asks God to inspect his heart and mind as if under a spiritual X-ray machine. David's invitation to God is a very healthy one. Remember, sin has a built-in tendency to conceal itself. Whenever we do something wrong, we immediately want to cover it up. Our heartache and pain is often repressed, swept under the rug. Our "dark side" is everything that must remain hidden to others, even to ourselves.

To God, however, nothing can remain hidden. That's why we can just as well open our heart up to God and let His bright light shine in! Yes, we can face our darkness, confess it, and deal with it. Living in God's light can only lead to forgiveness, healing, and communion. Why not?

Lord, You know me through and through.
Your love sets me free! Amen.

33

I am innocent, I am free

> I wash my hands in innocence and go around
> Your altar, O Lord, proclaiming thanksgiving
> aloud, and telling all Your wondrous deeds.
>
> PSALM 26:6-7

It's always wonderful to see how simply, directly, and personally David experienced his relationship with God. When he transgressed, he felt deep guilt and pleaded for forgiveness. Then, upon receiving pardon, he immediately had peace and felt his innocence renewed, as in this psalm.

Here David is convinced that peace has been restored between him and God, and it feels great! He is straightaway thanking and praising God! David has little of the neurotic guilt that we so often endure.

Remember that God's forgiveness is unconditional, powerful, and real. We are truly set free and truly free to feel at peace with God. That is the goal of our forgiveness.

Stop then with the endless feelings of guilt. Jesus gave His life so that you can put guilt down now. Walk in the freedom He bought you!

> Lord Jesus, thank You for setting
> me free. I am free indeed! Amen.

34

Your focus, your reality

> One thing have I asked of the Lord, that will I
> seek after: that I may dwell in the house of
> the Lord all the days of my life, to gaze upon the
> beauty of the Lord and to inquire in His temple.
>
> PSALM 27:4

Don't believe that faith is merely a matter of confessing correct doctrine. Solid doctrine is important, but faith is just as much a matter of the heart. If we never have any experience of God, if we nowhere find Him personally in our walk of faith, we really do not have enough.

There is absolutely no formula for experiencing God, because we can find Him in hundreds of ways: in ecstasy and silence, in joy and suffering. We need, however, to learn to experience God.

We need to focus on finding Him; we must intentionally become aware of Him. David, for example, stayed in God's house looking for Him, inquiring after Him, gazing upon His beauty. Remember, where your focus is, your reality will be.

*Lord, help me to look for You more,
to find You more – all around me! Amen.*

35
Loved, cared for, nurtured

> Even if my father and mother should
> desert me, You will take care of me.
> PSALM 27:10 (CEV)

One thing we should understand clearly: God really can be trusted with our well-being. We are not left alone in the universe, left to the mercy of "whatever." No, we are loved; we are cared for and nurtured; we are respected and valued.

David means that God will literally take care of him should his parents desert him. Jesus emphasized the same truth! Let's accept as a personal truth that we really can live carefree in this world. We often take up too much unneeded worry; we accept too many unnecessary responsibilities. Let them go – give them to God! Yes, release them, surrender them up!

Stop clinging to things that you cannot keep anyway. Forget a bit about your many needs and wants, and focus on God's grace – feel it like the sunshine on your face, and start to share that unconditional love with others.

Lord, I am so attached to my possessions, my needs, and my wants. I surrender them to You! Amen.

36

In this life, Lord!

I believe that I shall look upon the goodness of the LORD
in the land of the living! Wait for the LORD; be strong,
and let your heart take courage; wait for the LORD!

PSALM 27:13-14

David writes a wonderful psalm about God's provision and care. With God he feels safe and cared for. He is sure that he'll see the goodness of the Lord in the "land of the living" – that is to say in this life, in his immediate future!

Remember that David's faith was a very practical and tangible one. Therefore, he encourages the reader of his poem with certainty: trust in the Lord, be strong, take courage, and wait for the Lord!

Take David's advice as a personal promise. Expect the goodness of the Lord in this life. Trust God for it and wait on it – persevere until you have received it! The bonus is that in the next life you will be filled, saturated with God's goodness. With God you cannot lose!

> Lord, I am sure I will see Your
> goodness in my life – I am sure! Amen.

37
Favor for a lifetime

> For His anger is but for a moment, and His favor is for a lifetime. Weeping may tarry for the night, but joy comes with the morning.
>
> PSALM 30:5

The Israelites believed that God can become angry, but that His anger never lasts forever. In the end God would always forgive them because of His love. They reminded themselves of His covenant – one that He will never break. God's goodness will always overtake His anger! It's a beautiful thought, and it proved to be true.

But let's add some perspective:

- God's wrath is never rage – God never loses His temper. No, God's righteous anger is because of His demand for love, justice, and righteousness, and quite rightly so!
- God's emotions are never capricious or fickle. No, God is working according to His plan – and His plan for you will succeed!

In the New Testament we read that God's grace is a reality. His anger was directed at the cross for a moment so that His favor can be ours for a lifetime! Praise Him!

Lord, thank You for Your favor –
weeping will be followed by joy. Amen.

38

Live abundantly

What profit is there in my death, if I go down to the pit?
Will the dust praise You? Will it tell of Your faithfulness?

PSALM 30:9

David is writing here from an Old Testament perspective, which had little insight into an afterlife. Their concern was for the present. They believed that the dead was not aware enough to praise God; therefore, David wanted to live in order to praise the Lord!

Let's take from this the following truth: God wants us to live, truly and abundantly live. We were created to fully live to His glory. Live then! Embrace life completely, with all the good that it offers, as God's gift to you. Never say you shouldn't have lived or no longer want to live. Please never allow such thoughts into your mind – they are not God's will for you!

It is true that life – even a full and rewarding life – entails hardship and struggle. Yes, that's part of the deal, but ultimately life is worth living. Live with God and you will see for yourself.

Thank You, Lord, for an
abundant life with You. Amen.

39

In loving hands

Into Your hand I commit my spirit;
You have redeemed me, O LORD, faithful God.

PSALM 31:5

Once again we find David flat against the ground. He is in great distress and sorrow – grief is wasting him away; his eyes cannot cry anymore; his body is collapsing. It feels as if his years are filled with suffering.

He is absolutely desperate and despondent. Still, in this psalm we also hear another note. When David is done pouring his heart out, he declares his trust in God: "I trust in You, O Lord ... You are my God. My times are in Your hand" (Ps. 31:14-15). In verse five he sensitively writes, "Into Your hand I commit my spirit" – the very words Jesus repeated on the cross. How wonderful is this image!

Are you down, despairing? Then give your life into God's loving hands. The caring hands of your Father will carry you and guide you – and help you up again.

*Thank You, Lord, that my life and
my times are in Your loving hands. Amen.*

My hiding place

You are a hiding place for me; You preserve me
from trouble; You surround me with shouts of deliverance.

PSALM 32:7

How beautiful that God does not just supply a hiding place, He becomes a hiding place! Sometimes we just need to close the door behind us and let the world and all its demands go by.

Yes, sometimes we need to stop in the rush of things and give our soul a chance to catch up with our body, as it were. Where can we go when we have nowhere to go? We can go to God! He not only becomes our shelter but also gives us a song in our heart.

David says with God we are literally surrounded, encircled with songs of deliverance. When we hide with God it can mean to listen to songs of praise and victory, its truth sinking down into our soul and strengthening us. Perhaps David is referring to the singing of the angels around us, saying, "Your victory is assured!"

Thank You for the songs of victory around me, Lord!
Bring its message home into my heart! Amen.

41
God's plan

> But what the Lord has planned will
> stand forever. His thoughts never change.
> PSALM 33:11 (CEV)

This psalm proclaims that God is in full control. He made everything, He knows everyone, and He controls whatever happens. God destroys the schemes of sinners and implements His own plans instead.

Yes – God has plans! Ultimately, God's plans prevail, because God is God! He also has a plan for you and me! It's not a fixed, set program that ticks off like a clock, because we retain free will (within our limitations).

Rather, it's a built-in blueprint according to which we can develop. Discover God's plan for you by discovering who it is that God made. What is your personality? Your values and strengths? Your background and story? This – who you are – is what God made, and this – who you are – is what God wanted to use!

Flow with His design for your life, grow into His story for you! God's plan for you will succeed, believer, because God is working! Even in the events of today.

Lord, help me to grow into Your plan for my life. Amen.

42

The angel all around you

> The angel of the LORD encamps around
> those who fear Him, and delivers them.
>
> PSALM 34:7

*I*t's interesting to note that the Bible says the angel "encamps," or encircles (on all sides), those that serve Him. How is that possible? Well, God is spirit, and He can definitely camp in any or all of the dimensions that He wishes to! The point of Scripture here, however, is that those who serve God – or literally "fear" Him – will be protected from all sides.

No vulnerabilities will be left open! Yes, He is around us like the wall around an ancient city. Once again, to fear God is not to be afraid of Him (although God is a fearsome danger to His enemies) but to have reverence for Him, deep respect, and definite obedience. Just as for a father!

He will then protect you against the world – just as a father would – on all sides. Be assured of that today.

> Lord, be around me like a wall.
> Shelter me and save me! Amen.

43
The Lord is near

The Lord is near to the brokenhearted
and saves the crushed in spirit.

PSALM 34:18

Quite confidently David asserts, as if relating a spiritual law, that Jehovah is near to the brokenhearted, that He saves the "crushed of spirit," as is written in the Hebrew.

Yes, it is true: a broken heart attracts God; a crushed and defeated spirit draws Him as close as He can be! It is indeed a spiritual fact that brokenness brings us into the presence of God – especially brokenness before God.

Remember that God's character is to care and to love, to save. Therefore, God will not pass the brokenhearted by. He can never ignore the despairing spirit. He will not break the bruised reed and will not quench the flickering and dying wick (Isa. 42:3).

When you are at your lowest, God is at His nearest! Just turn around and see Him, just put out your hand and touch Him.

*Thank You, Lord, for being nearest
when I need You the most. Amen.*

His light

For with You is the fountain of life;
in Your light do we see light.

PSALM 36:9

If God did not switch on the light of the universe, there would still be only darkness. Light is electromagnetic waves travelling at 300 million meters per second. That's fast! Without light, of course, nothing would be seen – it's like taking a photograph in the dark.

Spiritually speaking it's also true: you and I have no inherent spirituality within us – by default we are dark and sinful. Nothing can happen in our lives unless God's light shines into our darkness. Only when the Holy Spirit broods over the void in our lives can creation occur. Only when God orders His light to shine can we start off as Christians – and only in His light can we grow as Christians.

That's why we need to read His Word, listen to His voice, and pay attention to His guidance all around us. Only in His light can we see the light, the psalmist says. Look for His light today!

Thank You, Lord, for Your light in my life.
Now I can know You! Amen.

45
Better is the little

Better is the little that the righteous
has than the abundance of many wicked.

PSALM 37:16

This psalm is about the paradox that godless people are more prosperous than the righteous. David struggles to understand it, just as we do! Still, we know that the world is not fair in this regard, because it's a broken and sinful world.

We also realize that judgment – God's great equalizer – is still ahead. In this verse David states that a righteous man's life is qualitatively better, even if he is poor, than the life of a godless person. It's the truth, but it forces us to rethink success. The world teaches us that success is to be wealthy, but the Bible teaches differently.

Success has to do with the sharing of love in our lives. Success is also to live with God – especially to experience His love, His peace, and His favor. Those who miss out on these things are the true losers – even if they're the richest people on earth.

*Lord, thank You for all the love in my life –
thank You for Your love! Amen.*

46

Hoping

> And so, Lord, where do I put
> my hope? My only hope is in You.
>
> PSALM 39:7 (NLT)

In this psalm David realizes that life is fleeting – even his own life is about to end. There is little hope left. That's how he feels! What can David do in his dark state? Where will he find hope? He finds his hope in God! The Message translates Psalm 39:7 as follows: "What am I doing in the meantime, Lord? Hoping, that's what I'm doing – hoping!" Let's take a lesson from David here. We so often put our hope in our circumstances. When things turn against us – and circumstances *will* be up and down – we feel without hope. Let's rather find our hope in the Lord, who made us to live a unique life, who loves us and will carry us through everything.

With God, life is always meaningful and hopeful, whatever the conditions. Also, with God the situation can change. Yes, quite so! Listen: with God you have every hope for a meaningful future!

> Lord, reveal Yourself to me again –
> reveal to me Your purpose! Amen.

47
Living praise

> He put a new song in my mouth, a song of praise to our God. Many will see and fear, and put their trust in the Lord.
>
> PSALM 40:3

David is rejoicing, because God saved him from danger. Now he has a "new song" in his mouth, meaning that he has a new reason to sing – he brings fresh praise!

Isn't it a sign of someone who lives close to God when there's always something new to praise God for? Such persons experience more of God, hear more from Him, see more of Him during their day. Take note that such a life isn't just meant for a few super spiritual saints. No, it's meant for every one of us!

We should wake up to it, open our eyes to God, and become aware of Him around us. When we live such a life of God's presence and involvement, the world will also see God – in us! Our lives will testify of His love and care and works. More reason for praise!

Lord, I want to live close to You.
I, too, want a new song to sing! Amen.

48

Reap and sow

> Blessed is the one who considers the poor!
> In the day of trouble the LORD delivers him.
>
> PSALM 41:1

Do you see the sow and reap principle in this verse? "Whatever one sows, that will he also reap," the Word says (Gal. 6:7). Some people take this the wrong way. They teach that one can sow in a certain way in order to reap in a certain way – as a method to receive personal blessings.

Such a view is not biblical, though, on several levels. Our walk with God is not primarily about what we can receive from Him but about what we can give Him, which is our life! Our focus should be on the sowing, and then God will take care of the reaping.

We can begin with the poor. We can start caring, especially where the need is overwhelming. Let's be Jesus to someone. That's what it's all about! Then, one day when we are weak and dependent ourselves, Jesus will be there for us.

> Lord Jesus, help me to be there for someone.
> You are always there for me! Amen.

49

Fear and faith

> Why are you cast down, O my soul, and why
> are you in turmoil within me? Hope in God;
> for I shall again praise Him, my salvation.
>
> PSALM 42:5

Don't we know this typical human struggle well? Like the psalmist in this verse, we quickly become "cast down" and "in turmoil" when we meet obstacles.

We become anxious so readily! But then again we are reminded of God. We resolve to trust again, to put our hope in Him. Yes, we know both fear and faith! We experience both the natural world and the supernatural. And we can grow in the struggle. See how it happens in this psalm: we catch ourselves doubting, and then we stop it. We reconfirm that we trust God as our helper, and we *confess* that we'll have reason to praise again. Do you see it?

Know your thoughts, and intervene when they are not productive or edifying anymore. Substitute them with positive and faith building truths! This is the transformation of the mind that the Bible talks about.

> Lord, help me to keep my thoughts on You:
> unwavering, trusting, believing. Amen.

50

Grab hold of God

> Awake! Why are You sleeping, O Lord? Rouse Yourself!
> Do not reject us forever! Why do You hide Your face?
> Why do You forget our affliction and oppression?
>
> PSALM 44:23-24

Wow, what straightforward words are these – directed to God? What are we to make of them? Remember, this is not temperamental old David reacting from his personal anguishes. No, this psalm was an established part of the Korahite temple choir's repertoire. It was often sung!

The people of biblical times were direct and upfront, as Mediterranean people still are today. They didn't hide their emotions – it just spilled over! Similarly, their relationship with God was experienced as intensely emotional and deeply personal. Let's learn this from them, then: *full* commitment, total involvement, deep relationship! We, as modern people, are often emotionally repressed and shy away from deep expression. That's why we often end with a shallow spirituality.

Why are we so halfhearted? Listen – do you have a need? Grab hold of God with everything you have!

Lord, I grab onto You with my whole heart:
with my full understanding, feeling, and will! Amen.

51

Not lovable – loving

> The King will greatly desire your beauty;
> because He is your Lord, worship Him.
> PSALM 45:11 (NKJV)

In this verse, the psalm about the king of Israel now turns to his queen. The chosen princess will become his bride. A wonderful wedding is described, filled with beauty, glory, and honor. This psalm has been understood as Messianic since early times, because the king is addressed here in exalted, even divine terms.

Christ is the ultimate King, and we – His church – are His bride! The question we need to ponder is why the King would choose us as His bride. Aren't humans known to be self-centered and contrary – at their best, not very lovable? Indeed, we are! So, what does the King see in us? We truly don't know, but Scripture confirms that the King does desire us for Himself.

Yes, He loves us. He seeks us out. He finds us and commits to us. The better answer to our question would lie not in our lovability but in His love and absolute grace.

Thank You, Lord, for Your love!
The glory belongs to You. Amen.

52

Be still

> Be still, and know that I am God. I will be exalted
> among the nations, I will be exalted in the earth!
> PSALM 46:10

This psalm is about the chaos and uncertainty of this world. Nations threaten each other, wars loom, storms rage. We mustn't be anxious, however. With God we are safe and secure.

He is exalted high above the tumult and clamor of the world. He wants us to realize this truth and relax. The word that is used here for "be still" means to let go, to release, to relax the tension. It means to stop trying, to put it down. Somewhere along the way we have tried enough, stressed enough, worried enough. It's time to give up. Let it go! Be still, says God, and quiet down.

Know that God is on the scene. He is in control! Let God be God. Let Him do the God business. Leave it to Him, whatever happens. Let Him do what He wants to do. Surrender now. Be still.

> Lord, there are things that only You can do.
> I stand back and leave it to You. Amen.

53

Praise is your calling

Clap your hands, all peoples!
Shout to God with loud songs of joy!

PSALM 47:1

This beautiful psalm by the Korahites describes God as the King of the whole earth. He is crowned in glory and all peoples should come and worship Him. Remember that the purpose of Israel's election was to be the light of the world, to be a model people. In them, the whole world should have seen a nation serving the true God and been invited to serve Him as well.

The Jews were often reluctant with this commission, but it nonetheless happened when their Messiah came. Through Jesus Christ believers from all nations of the earth are now worshiping the one true God, the God of Israel. The New Testament teaches that we, the non-Jewish believers, have joined with the Jewish believers and have become one covenant people.

Praise God, then – clap your hands, rejoice, shout to the King of the earth! Remember, to praise God is also a discipline; therefore this verse is a command, not a request.

*God of Israel, I praise You for
including me in Your people! Amen.*

54

The golden city

> Great is the LORD and greatly to be praised
> in the city of our God! His holy mountain,
> beautiful in elevation, is the joy of all the earth.
>
> PSALM 48:1-2

In biblical times, Jerusalem was much smaller, but still beautiful: on Mount Zion in the crisp highlands of Judea, the Kidron brook flowing by, the Pool of Siloam supplying ample water surrounded by fields, gardens, and hills. Within the walls were the royal palace and other state buildings, and on the highest peak, of course, God's impressive temple. There, in the Holy of Holies, the presence of God rested. Wonderful! Even so, this beautiful city is only a symbol of the eternal Jerusalem that is coming.

When the King of kings comes to be with His people forever – and He is on His way – the presence of God will fill the earth from side to side, according to the Bible (Rev. 21:23). The whole earth will become one big sanctuary, one big temple. Wait for the New Jerusalem – then you'll see true beauty!

Lord Jesus, come! Come be with us. Amen.

55

Souls from Sheol

But God will ransom my soul from
the power of Sheol, for He will receive me.

PSALM 49:15

The people of the Old Testament had a limited view of eternal life. They believed that the righteous would have their reward and the sinners their punishment in this life.

When you died, you went – according to them – to Sheol, a bleak place where you existed as a mere shadow. The phantoms who lived there either slept or moved about weakly. True, colorful, and vital life was to be had while on earth. Yet, in this psalm we find an expectation that God would save the psalmist's soul from Sheol and "receive" him. How beautiful!

The New Testament confirms that Christ has indeed ransomed every believer from death. We will also be received by our Savior, and our lives will continue with Him – vitally and eternally! We'll meet each other before God's throne!

*Father, You so loved me that You sent Your only
Son so that I, who believe in Him, shall not perish
but have eternal life (John 3:16). Thank You! Amen.*

56

The meaning of it

Be not afraid when a man becomes rich, when the
glory of his house increases. For when he dies he will
carry nothing away; his glory will not go down after him.

PSALM 49:16-17

We live in a very materialistic society. Money is our main purpose, to buy and consume is our ideal. Wealth dictates our success or failure in this world.

The biblical message, however, is the opposite. No one warns about the dangers of money as much as Jesus did. He says money can easily become an idol (Matt. 6:24). Money can easily come between us and God. We should take His message to heart, because material wealth is *not* the meaning of life.

According to the Bible, the successful person is not the one who made money but the one who loved. Less well-to-do people with warm hearts and warm relationships are more successful than well-off people in cold and empty houses. Yes, love is the meaning of life. Show love – there is so little time!

Lord, give me a life of love. Help me to love! Amen.

57

Only one

> The Mighty One, God the LORD, speaks and summons
> the earth from the rising of the sun to its setting.
>
> PSALM 50:1

This psalm starts off interestingly with some of God's names: *El*, *Elohim*, and *Yahweh*. Here *El* is translated as "the Mighty One", *Elohim* means "the God of Israel", and *Yahweh* is "the Lord".

This repetition underlines and intensifies the fact that Israel's God, *Yahweh*, is the only true God. Let's remember that! We live in a world of many religions, and we treat each with the utmost respect. That is very important. Still, we hold to our belief that there is only one true God. All gods and all faiths are not equal. There is only one true God, the God of Israel, and only one Savior, the Lord Jesus Christ!

There is only one true faith and that is the one confessing the above. With great conviction Christians call on the whole world, from east to west, to accept Christ as Savior. Keep your faith – be strong. And don't forget to love!

Lord, keep me faithful and give me a heart of love. Amen.

How wonderful

Call upon Me in the day of trouble;
I will deliver you, and you shall glorify Me.

PSALM 50:15

God is taking His people to task. They did sacrifice to Him but their hearts were not with Him. He now reminds them that He already owns all the cattle on all the hills and does not have a need for sacrificial animals.

The sacrificial system was merely a vehicle for them to express their heart's devotion and their gratitude to Him. More than all their sacrifices, God asks His people three things: (1) a praise-offering meant from the heart, (2) that they keep the vows made in His name and then, surprisingly, (3) that they call upon Him in their need.

How wonderful is this? The sacrifice God asks for is the chance to be God to them – to prove Himself as the great God that He is! Shall we take God up on His invitation? Yes, we shall. Thank You, Lord!

Lord Jesus, accept my sacrifice of praise for what You have done! Then I offer You my need. Deliver me, Lord! Amen.

59

I have sinned

> You are really the one I have sinned against;
> I have disobeyed You and have done wrong.
>
> PSALM 51:4 (CEV)

David is confessing his sin. He had an affair with one of his soldiers' wives and then organized for the man to be killed in battle. When he says that he sinned against God "only," he doesn't mean that he committed nothing against a fellow man. He means that he realizes that his sin against another has brought him into direct conflict with God.

Let's consider the following: sin can never be swept under the rug. We cannot just decide to do better the next time around or turn over a new leaf. No, sin is a matter between God and us, and it must be sorted out with God. It must be acknowledged to God and confessed.

God's light must shine on it. The Holy Spirit must be involved to help you grow away from those things. Live your life in a spiritual way, not in a worldly way.

Lord, there are things that cannot remain the way they are. Help me with the following … Amen.

Cleansing and contacts

> Purge me with hyssop, and I shall be clean;
> wash me, and I shall be whiter than snow.
>
> PSALM 51:7

Ritual purity is a central concept in the Old Testament law. Purity led to communion with others and worthiness before God. Many, many regulations covered this topic and had much to do with avoiding unclean things: unclean food, unclean people, or unclean items.

Temporary impurity could be resolved by a ritual or a sacrifice, but some people – like lepers or heathens – were permanently impure. In these verses David – because of his sin – feels deeply unclean and completely cut off from God. He desperately needs God to cleanse him, to "unsin" him as is literally stated.

In the New Testament, however, we live by faith in the cleansing blood of Christ, which permanently brought us into communion with God. We are clean because of Him, but we also want to be clean for Him. To that purpose, it remains useful to remember that impurity is transmitted by contact.

> Lord, help me not to become stained
> by that which is impure. Amen.

61

Don't throw me away

> Cast me not away from Your presence,
> and take not Your Holy Spirit from me.
>
> PSALM 51:11

David is deeply convicted of his sin and is pleading for forgiveness. It feels as if God is far away. He therefore begs God not to reject him.

His fear is that he might lose his kingship. He asks God not to withdraw His Spirit from him, since the Holy Spirit was given in the Old Testament to certain anointed people like kings, prophets, or priests. David, for example, was filled by the Spirit at the moment of his crowning as king. Is he going to lose it all now? From our New Testament perspective, we believe that the Holy Spirit is not easily withdrawn from believers, but we are warned not to "grieve" the Holy Spirit (Eph. 4:30) or even to "quench" Him (1 Thess. 5:19).

One can indeed live a life in which there is, practically speaking, no place for God's Spirit. What will the end of such a life be?

> Holy Spirit, be with me! I pray that
> my behavior will never grieve You. Amen.

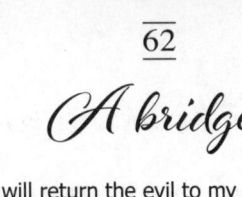

62

A bridge

> He will return the evil to my enemies;
> in Your faithfulness put an end to them.
>
> PSALM 54:5

Here we have the biblical principle of sowing and reaping again. What you do to others will be returned to you. David's prayer that God must destroy his enemies may sound strange to us, but it fits into this principle when correctly understood.

Take note that it's the enemies' own evil that is returned to them, not God's evil intentions. The effects of sin are part of the sin – and sometimes it hangs around long after the sin has passed! God allows it as He allowed sin, together with its consequences, since Adam and Eve. It's part of our freedom to choose.

If you dig holes for others, the consequence will be that there are holes around you – which you will fall into yourself. It's best not to dig holes! Rather, build bridges for others – bridges for you to cross as well. Leave the punishing to God.

Lord, help me to give encouragement, love, and peace.
On the day of need it will return to me. Amen.

63

Handle the pressure

> I am restless in my complaint and I moan,
> because of the noise of the enemy,
> because of the oppression of the wicked.
>
> PSALM 55:2-3

David's best friend has betrayed him. David cannot sleep, and his heart feels heavy.

The word translated here as "oppression" can also mean pressure. The bad news presses onto David, in other words. Pressure is actually a mechanical term referring to a force that is exercised against a physical system. If the system cannot adequately handle it, the tension (or stress) inside the system increases – eventually it can break. This can also happen to the human system. If undue expectations and responsibilities are laden onto us, we can feel the stress increasing. If we cannot bear it, something must give way.

What can you do? Well, the stress must be reduced. There is no other way. Don't just pray – do something about your stress load. Negotiate with those involved, and rid yourself of some of the burden. Working off stress by exercising and intentional relaxation also helps.

Heavenly Father, I feel stressed!
Show me how to handle it. Amen.

64

Run from it

> Oh, that I had wings like a dove! I would fly
> away and be at rest; yes, I would wander
> far away; I would lodge in the wilderness.
>
> PSALM 55:6-7

David is feeling anxious. His friends are now his enemies! He's restless and fearful, his heart is cringing inside of him, and his body is trembling.

That's exactly how anxiety and fear feel. David says he wishes he could just escape to the wilderness where he can find peace and rest. This is typical, isn't it? We have similar desperate ideas of running away from it all. The good news is that we can actually run away, spiritually speaking. The desert to which so many men of God have retreated is available to all of us, because it resides in the heart.

There, deep in the spirit, we find the quiet place where the Holy Spirit lives, where we can have our peace and rest. Remember to regularly go to that place, because it takes practice to find it!

*Lord, help me to find peace amidst the
throng and the noise – help me to find You! Amen.*

65

Throw your cares away

Cast your burden on the Lord, and He will sustain you;
He will never permit the righteous to be moved.

PSALM 55:22

We can get to the point where we're so discouraged or frustrated with our problems that we would rather take the lot and throw them in the bin – if it were only possible! Have you ever gotten to that point?

Now God is saying that it is possible. We can throw our burdens – the unbearable emotional load of our problems – onto Him. We cannot ignore the problem itself or avoid the responsibility it brings, but without so much of the burden it becomes lighter, more bearable, manageable. Give your burdens to God in prayer one by one. Then make a firm decision not to be anxious about them anymore.

Whenever anxious thoughts arise, identify them as unwelcome, and exchange them for strong confessions of faith. It's an active deed: a decision, a release, a refusal, a willful exchange. Be strict with yourself – intentionally build your faith!

*Lord Jesus, I now cast the following burdens
onto You ... Take them away, Lord. Amen.*

66

Your jar of tears

You have kept count of my tossings; put my tears
in Your bottle. Are they not in Your book?

PSALM 56:8

What a surprising verse! It underlines the fact that God notices our tears and that they matter to Him deeply.

Can we say something about crying today? To cry is natural, normal, and good for us. It releases toxins and stress hormones. Crying relieves stress better and faster than many medicines, yet we are so reluctant to cry. We were taught to contain our emotions – especially men believe that "cowboys don't cry." Let's make it clear that the people of biblical times weren't so inhibited. They cried when they wanted to cry – the men as well!

David often wept, and believed that God counted his tears. Jesus wept, as did many of the faith heroes and spiritual fathers. Learn to release your emotions, release your tears – have a good cry when you need it. Remember, God knows about the heartache you suffer – He weeps with you!

Thank You, Lord, for knowing my tears. Every tear
is treasured by You. How beautiful You are! Amen.

67

God is on my side

> Then my enemies will turn back in the day
> when I call. This I know, that God is for me.
>
> PSALM 56:9

David says, "God is for me." It's a powerful statement, but isn't it a bit presumptuous? Isn't God on everyone's side? Does David want to hijack God all for himself?

Remember, Old Testament believers felt that if they kept God's law they were right with God. For them, God would certainly be on the side of the godly – never on the side of the godless! Remember also that David had an absolutely personal relationship with God. He spoke with God, heard His voice, and lived with the full knowledge of God's presence and involvement.

For David, success meant God's blessing and failure meant God's displeasure. What do these things mean to us? Well, Christ's death proves that God is most definitely on your side – very personally so! He died for you. There is really no one who is more on your side than God!

*Lord, I live today in the knowledge that
You are wholly and completely for me! Amen.*

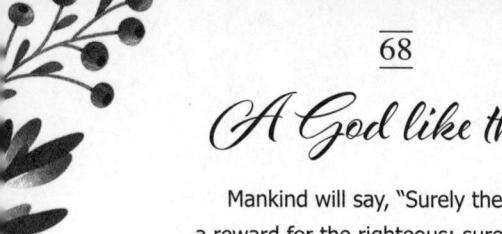

68

A God like that

> Mankind will say, "Surely there is
> a reward for the righteous; surely there
> is a God who judges on earth."
>
> PSALM 58:11

In this psalm David sets himself against evil people. He prays that God will judge them and even suggests some punishments!

Jesus of course taught us otherwise, but statements like these come from a deep sense of righteousness and justice. Evil people must not get away with their misdeeds. Of course God isn't a God who will let evil people get away with everything. If that were true, the whole system of justice would fall apart. No, the full retribution and punishment of sin has been handed to Christ, and justice was fully served. Those who accept that in faith can have the benefit of full pardon.

So, there is a God "who judges on earth" – there is punishment and there is reward. Leave your matters with Him. Let Him judge whom He wants to judge, and let Him show mercy where He wants to show mercy.

*Lord, You are the judge,
the perfect judge – not me. Amen.*

69

Let the sun rise

> But I will sing of Your strength; I will sing aloud of
> Your steadfast love in the morning. For You have been
> to me a fortress and a refuge in the day of my distress.
>
> PSALM 59:16

*I*n the night, David sees people lurking around his house. They were sent by Saul, possibly to prevent him from escaping, because Saul distrusted and hated him.

David describes these ominous figures as a pack of dogs that prowl around, growling, showing their teeth. They make him feel anxious, and he pleads to God for protection. Then, in this verse, the new day has dawned and the enemy is nowhere to be seen. The fear and foreboding of the night hour is a mere memory. Isn't this typical?

During the night everything seems so much worse – the darkness so easily produces the worst-case scenario! Don't make big decisions in the literal or figurative night. Wait for the day. Let God's light shine on it first.

*Lord, when it's dark in my life, give me faith
and patience to see through to the dawn. Amen.*

Certainty in uncertainty

From the end of the earth I call to You when my heart is faint. Lead me to the rock that is higher than I, for You have been my refuge, a strong tower against the enemy.

PSALM 61:2-3

David is calling to God, for he is anxious and fearful. He says he's calling to God "from the end of the earth," because that is how he feels – as if God is far, far away.

David has a great need for security, for certainty, and he therefore asks to be led to "the rock that is higher than I." In other words, to something that exceeds his own power, and powerlessness. According to the church fathers, that rock is Jesus Christ.

Do you also feel uncertain, anxious, apprehensive about the future? Do not fear, because Jesus knows your future. He is speaking to you from the future, telling you that He has the future under control. He is your safe place, your strength, your Rock – your future! You will not go under.

Lord Jesus, bring quiet to my heart.
Give me peace. Be my Rock! Amen.

71

My soul follows hard

> My soul clings to You; Your right hand upholds me.
> PSALM 63:8

The King James Version of the Bible is beautiful when it says my soul "followeth hard after Thee." David is implying that his soul is adhering, clinging – that he is stuck on God!

Let's unpack a bit what it means to follow God so intensely. First, we notice that David's soul is not longing after the world but after God. That's important! How does one seek "hard" after God, practically speaking? It means that we find time for Him, that we want to pray, that we are eager to learn about God's Word, and that we really want to be obedient. To follow closely means to want to be where God is. We find the converse true as well: God stays near to him, God follows him, God "cleaves" to him!

God's "right hand" holds David near and carries him. So, a very, very close relationship is described. The lesson is this: seek after God, and God will seek after you!

> Lord, I do have a longing for You.
> Help me to find You! Amen.

72

Hearer and answerer

Our God, You deserve praise in Zion,
where we keep our promises to You. Everyone
will come to You because You answer prayer.

PSALM 65:1-2 (CEV)

In this psalm David rejoices because God has answered their prayers!

It is indeed wonderful to pray and then experience God's answer. It makes us feel that our prayers are working. Still, it doesn't always go as we expect, because our idea of how prayer should work is often wrong. It's not wrong for our prayers to be answered just like we ask, but we often ask the wrong things. God's perspective is different from ours, and although He hears everything we ask for, He responds the way He wants to respond.

Luckily, in Scripture we read that the Holy Spirit improves our prayers by interceding for us "according to the will of God" (Rom. 8:26-27). His prayers (in us) are then answered exactly as asked! From our side, prayer is mainly to lay our life at God's feet and then to simply trust Him with it.

Lord, I boldly ask You and simply
trust You. Your will is best! Amen.

73
Fire and water

We went through fire and through water;
yet You have brought us out to a place of abundance.

PSALM 66:12

The poet's mind wanders to a specific time when Israel endured extreme hardship – wondering perhaps if that contradicts God's power. He might be thinking of their slavery in Egypt or of the time the Assyrians besieged Jerusalem for two years. Yes, those were terrible times when they went "through fire and through water."

Where was this awesome and powerful God then? Then comes the climax. God saved them from all of that and brought them again into abundance! Their experience teaches us that there *will* be fire and there *will* be water.

Challenges, stress, and heartache are a part of life. Remember, though, that we move through these things – that they come, are endured, and they pass away. They are temporary, in other words; they're passing. This is God's promise! After the crises, there will be abundance again – joy, peace, love. There will be!

*Heavenly Father, I know that life entails
good and bad. I also know that life ends
with You, who are the ultimate good! Amen.*

I know Him

For I cried out to Him for help, praising Him as I spoke.
PSALM 66:17 (NLT)

In this verse the poet tells us of two actions: first he cried to God, and then he followed it up with praise.

From out of his prayer, his praise directly flowed. He did not praise because God had answered him. No, his praise flowed out before God could answer. He praised God just because he knew God! He knew his God could be trusted with his petition, his needs, his life. He praised God in advance for His intervention, but also just for who God is. What a lesson! To know God is to love Him and to trust Him, because our experience with Him teaches us that.

So get to know God. In closure, do you have a need, a cry in your heart? Pray to your God and praise Him straightforwardly for it, for He is already busy in your life. Yes, He is present and He is deeply involved.

> Lord, I leave my need with You now.
> I trust You, because I know You. Amen.

75

Prepare and rejoice!

> Sing to God, sing praises to His name;
> lift up a song to Him who rides through the deserts;
> His name is the LORD; exult before Him!
>
> PSALM 68:4

In this psalm the coming of the Lord is described. Where He comes, the enemy is defeated – every knee bows before Him! As Christians we see this in Jesus' coming.

Remember, He is already on His way. When Christ comes, we as His children have definite tasks. We need to prepare for Him by getting our lives in order so that we can meet with Him confidently. Also, we need to declare to the world that our God is coming, so that they can also be prepared. Finally, we can start rejoicing because our salvation is near, because everything will end well with Him, because we will be loved forever!

Rejoicing prepares our hearts and prepares the way for His coming, spiritually speaking. It is a powerful act of faith to rejoice – it makes us spiritually stronger, and that's a fact.

Lord, I am excited over You and Your coming.
I will begin singing Your praises! Amen.

76

Lose control

> I sink in deep mire, where there is no foothold; I have come into deep waters, and the flood sweeps over me.
>
> PSALM 69:2

David is desperately calling out to God. He feels as if a strong stream has taken hold of him. The water is already at his neck, and his feet are losing their grip. It's terrifying!

Yes, how terrible to feel that you are losing control in your circumstances. Sometimes things just happen and take you along: Management makes a decision; the results are in, and they're not good. Or economic or political changes affect you negatively. Remember, if there is something that you can do about such things, you should surely do it. In many circumstances, things can be turned around. Then again, there are things about which you can do nothing – absolutely nothing!

Don't despair, though. Resist the feeling that you're going to sink. You will not! Faithfully and willfully surrender your circumstances to God. Trust Him who is still in control! He will carry you through.

Almighty God, circumstances are against me, but You are strong! Amen.

77

Not too far?

> It is for Your sake alone that I am insulted
> and blush with shame. I am like a stranger to
> my relatives and like a foreigner to my own family.
> PSALM 69:7-8 (CEV)

David mentions something that we also encounter. He says his desire to serve God fully is not understood by his family and friends. In our day, we have freedom of religion, and many are nominally Christian, but the moment you really want to live differently, it causes problems. Then people say you're taking things too far.

Let's be very honest: Christians must live wisely in this world. It's of no use to fret because unbelievers look at us and are completely put off. No, that would miss the point completely.

Let's live inspiring lives that are filled with love, joy, peace, and faith. That is what others must see. Our walk with God entails choices that will be unpopular with others. That's just how it's going to be – we will be pleasing God first.

*Lord, help me to live wisely in this world,
and help me to put You first in all things. Amen.*

78

Pray it and praise it

> May all who seek You rejoice and
> be glad in You! May those who love
> Your salvation say evermore, "God is great!"
>
> PSALM 70:4

David is seeking God's help again. Let's have a closer look at his approach, though. First he describes his dire circumstances and urgent requests to God.

To pour out your heart to God has the advantage of externalizing and objectifying your problem. It is talked out and, as such, becomes more understandable and manageable. Try writing out your prayers, and you'll see.

Second David praises God for His intervention, as in this verse. Most of his psalms end in this way. Take note that David offers praise before his prayers are answered. He praises not because God already answered but – as an act of faith – because God will answer.

You and I can also learn to praise God, to trust God, to surrender to God, to find peace in God before any prayer has been answered – in faith! Faith works before God works. Faith changes things, and it changes us!

> Lord, teach me to praise You
> regardless of anything else. Amen.

79

Generation to generation

May they fear You while the sun endures,
and as long as the moon, throughout all generations!

PSALM 72:5

Solomon is praying for God to protect the king, so that righteousness and peace can reign and God be served "throughout all generations."

Let's explore this last idea. The current generation got their faith from their parents but have embraced it as their own. You, for example, are in a personal relationship with God. Your child is watching all this: she sees you praying, living in faith, and speaking about God. Later on she will decide whether she wants that faith as her own.

Your example, and others', is extremely important in this regard! When she does take it up as her personal faith, she will for herself seek God and live according to her beliefs – then later on her own children's eyes will watch her being a Christian. That's how it works. Our faith is not so much taught as caught, as they say.

Lord, let me live in such a way that my children will want to accept You as their God! Amen.

80

The turning point

But when I thought how to understand this,
it seemed to me a wearisome task, until I went into
the sanctuary of God; then I discerned their end.

PSALM 73:16-17

Asaph got stuck in his faith. He is wondering whether it's worth serving God. It seems that the godless are well off, while the God-fearing are struggling!

He gets to a turning point, however. He says it remained a burden to him "until I went into the sanctuary of God." There's the answer! Meeting with God about the problem makes all the difference. In fact, a true encounter with God changes your whole perspective, your attitude, your goals, your life's meaning – everything! Do you identify with Asaph? Does it burden your faith to live among unbelievers? Do you wonder whether they might be right not to believe after all? Do you?

Go, then, again to your God, in His sanctuary, whether it be in your quiet time, your worship, at church, or wherever. That is something unbelievers can never do – and it will make all the difference!

Lord, I do have such a longing for You! Amen.

81

The other way

> When my soul was embittered, when I was
> pricked in heart, I was brutish and ignorant;
> I was like a beast toward You.
>
> PSALM 73:21-22

Asaph was bitter over the many sinful people who apparently did so well. He asked, "Why isn't God punishing them?"

Afterward, though, he realized his mistake: He wanted God to set everything right now. Unfortunately, things do not work that way. In fact, they work the other way around: God puts His hand on your shoulder and drafts you into His service. He wants you to follow Him and serve Him. He is asking certain things from you and is now waiting on your answer! He promises much blessing for you, but ultimately it's not about your comfort or wealth. Ultimately, it's about God's plan and God's glory.

So, let's get past our own will and declare ourselves available for His will. Do not concern yourself too much about everything that hasn't been set right as yet. It will be set right, but in due course.

> Lord, forgive me. I sometimes think
> it's all about me. It's all about You! Amen.

82

Both, you know

> It is God who executes judgment,
> putting down one and lifting up another.
> PSALM 75:7

It is arrogant to boast that you're a "self-made person," because most often this is just not the case.

Research has shown that success seldom arises from a vacuum – it mostly stands on the family's knowledge, experience, money, or connections, on the privilege of having had a good education or on opportunities that came your way. What others would call good fortune, we as believers would call grace, or God's favor. Let's not be arrogant, the poet says. Let's be humble. It's up to God to decide who rises and who falls! Of course we should work hard to attain something, because from our side that's the way to success.

However, we should also pray, because not everything is in our hands. Both of these aspects are important: praying and working! Remember that we cannot work what we should have prayed, or pray what we should have worked. There's a distinction.

Lord, thank You for Your grace and blessing.
My hard work is nothing without that! Amen.

83

It is God

> In Judah God is known; His name is great
> in Israel. His abode has been established
> in Salem, His dwelling place in Zion.
>
> PSALM 76:1-2

Asaph is rejoicing over the Lord. He says God is "known" in Judah, with the grammar suggesting that God has made Himself to be known in Judah.

It's a biblical truth that we would have known nothing of God if He hadn't revealed Himself to us. We only know Him insofar as He has made Himself known. This happens to us in a very personal way. We carry on with our lives – without God – until we realize that His hand is resting on our shoulder. It happens in many ways: by hearing the Word, by our circumstances forcing us to think, by an inner discontent that will not go away. At first we might not relate these things to God.

Eventually, however, we may realize that it's Him! Yes, God is speaking to You indeed – even through this message He is calling out to You! Will you listen?

Heavenly Father, these things that are happening, is it You? What are You saying? Amen.

84

Great enough

> I will ponder all Your work, and meditate
> on Your mighty deeds. Your way, O God,
> is holy. What god is great like our God?
>
> PSALM 77:12-13

Asaph is greatly troubled and pleads with God for an answer. He prays and prays, but nothing happens. That's how this psalm begins.

In the second part, Asaph asks a lot of questions. Where is the God who does wonders? Why isn't He answering? What about His steadfast love? Did He forget to be gracious? Then, in the last part of the psalm, Asaph merely reflects on God's greatness. That's how this psalm ends – as if Asaph is just leaving his problem with the Mighty God. He can deal with it, and He can be trusted with it.

How it's going to happen Asaph doesn't know, but that's not important. The God who could take His people through the sea can take an individual through his problems! We can also leave our troubles with the Great God, with the Almighty. He is great enough for it.

*Lord, You know me, and You know my challenges.
I trust You with them all. Amen.*

85

Go and celebrate!

> Blow the trumpet at the new moon, at the
> full moon, on our feast day. For it is a statute
> for Israel, a rule of the God of Jacob.
>
> PSALM 81:3-4

Asaph calls up the people: the feast, probably of Tabernacles, is about to begin! The Feast of Tabernacles is a joyful harvest festival that also celebrates the Jews' deliverance from Egypt.

It happens only five days after the most solemn and holy Day of Atonement, so the change in tone is considerable. Anyway, when the shofar is blown, the people must join with joyful hearts. You know, there is a time to fast and a time to feast. Both are important, and both are God's command.

Some Christians cannot relax or celebrate at all – they feel it's unfitting. That's wrong! God's children must absolutely be able to enjoy life, and to celebrate exuberantly. To celebrate life is a gift from God that we may not refuse. So, do not be ungrateful – there are so many reasons to celebrate!

Lord, thank You that I may enjoy the life You've given, that You grant me true happiness! Amen!

Open up wide

> I am the Lord your God, who brought you up out of
> the land of Egypt. Open your mouth wide, and I will fill it.
>
> PSALM 81:10

The Lord made a covenant with His people at Sinai: if they served God fully, God would fully provide their needs.

In *our* verse, we read a particularly poignant and meaningful perspective on the covenant from God's own mouth: "I am the Lord your God … Open your mouth wide, and I will fill it." The reference of course is to baby birds who open their beaks wide for their parents to put food in. This image of fledglings illustrates our complete dependence on God and emphasizes that we should look up to Him with great expectation and trust.

Take note, though, God does not just give. We should also actively receive. God provides, but faith is to ask for it, to patiently wait for it, and then to take it from His hand. Develop your faith while you wait.

Father, I have such a great expectation from You.
Provide in my need, in Jesus' name! Amen.

87
Milk and honey

> But I would feed you with the finest bread
> and with the best honey until you were full.
> PSALM 81:16 (CEV)

In this psalm the people are called to the Feast of Tabernacles. The feast celebrates how God provided for His people in the desert, in every way. Still, their true goal was Canaan, the "land of milk and honey" (Exod. 3:8).

God's ultimate intention with them was the promised blessing and abundance! This is God's goal for us as well, but we are often like the Israelites, spiritually wandering in the desert. Let's put it like this: a desert life isn't a life without struggles, but a life without God. It's where we really try to be in control.

That can never lead to God's promises! In this verse God says that the "finest bread" and the "best honey" is found with Him – nowhere else. He affords us provision and sustenance, milk and honey! Listen, if you cannot find your Canaan in Him, you will never find Canaan anywhere.

Lord, You are the living water, the bread of life. You satisfy and fulfill! Amen.

88

Show me your love

> Give justice to the weak and the fatherless; maintain the right of the afflicted and the destitute. Rescue the weak and the needy; deliver them from the hand of the wicked.
>
> PSALM 82:3-4

Sometimes we get so spiritual that we forget the purpose of it all. We become completely focused on our relationship with Jesus, on studying the Word, praying, praising God, ministering with our gifts, and so on.

We can easily become sidelined, however, when our whole spiritual life starts to revolve around me: me and my blessing, me and my ministry, me and my walk with God. It can also happen that we consider ourselves ahead of others, spiritually speaking. Take note that true spirituality leads to transformation, a change of heart.

In fact, spirituality translates into love. Love is the fruit, the result! And remember, love is a practical and visible thing. It has to do with helping the weak, the parentless, the destitute. Read the verse again. The world says, "Don't show me your spirituality – show me your love!"

Lord, help me bear the fruit
of the spiritual walk – love! Amen.

89

Springs start flowing

> You bless all who depend on You for their strength
> and all who deeply desire to visit Your temple.
> When they reach Dry Valley, springs start flowing,
> and the autumn rain fills it with pools of water.
>
> PSALM 84:5-6 (CEV)

Blessed are those who depend on God for strength. Such people have "highways to Zion" in their hearts, meaning that they often think of going to Jerusalem again.

They long for the city of God, because they long for God! There – with Him – they will renew their strength. If they go through dry spells in their lives, they will find inner springs opening up to carry them through. The application is self-evident: the sanctuary of God is not in Jerusalem anymore, but in our hearts, where the Spirit of God dwells.

Blessed are you when you find God there! He will become a fountain in your heart – as Jesus promised – that will carry you through the most difficult of times. His strength will become your strength. Yes, find that strength!

> Lord, I so need Your strength. Open up
> Your fountains in me! Amen.

90

Houses without God

> One day in Your temple is better than a thousand
> anywhere else. I would rather serve in Your
> house, than live in the homes of the wicked.
>
> PSALM 84:10 (CEV)

Today, there are many homes where God isn't welcome, where His name is never mentioned. Sometimes believers live in such a house. Perhaps the mother serves God, but the father does not – or their children are rebellious.

Other times, again, a child is the only believer in a house, faithfully praying for her parents. Let's make Joshua's decision our own: "As for me and my house, we will serve the Lord" (Josh. 24:15).

Do not hesitate to give God His place in your home. Talk about Him. Pray when you want to pray. Let your family see that you read the Bible. Do not let your home become a cold and indifferent house without God. No, make it a house of God!

> Lord, be welcome in our home.
> We want to serve You! Amen.

91

My sun and shield

> For the Lord God is a sun and shield; the Lord
> bestows favor and honor. No good thing does
> He withhold from those who walk uprightly.
>
> PSALM 84:11

The Korahites, who wrote this song about the temple – "How lovely is Your dwelling place" (Ps. 84:1) – now end it with a beautiful blessing.

This is the psalm's conclusion. Remember, in this psalm it's not so much about love for the outward temple, but love and longing for the God who can be found in the temple. Such a longing is always rewarded with a blessing! Do you also long for God – do you seek after Him? Remember, when we seek we will find (Matt. 7:7); when we draw near to God, He will draw near to us (James 4:8).

Yes, when we take a step in His direction, He will take two steps in ours! Oh, and when you have found God, you have found the greatest blessing this universe can offer! In Him all the good things of this life can be found.

> "Lord of hosts, blessed is the one
> who trusts in You" (Ps. 84:12). Amen.

92

Revive me

> Will You not revive us again, that Your people
> may rejoice in You? Show us Your steadfast love,
> O Lord, and grant us Your salvation.
>
> PSALM 85:6-7

In this psalm the Korahites feel as if God is far away. Where is the God that used to live with His people?

That's why they pray for God to revive them again – for Him to restore their joy. Revival can only be experienced by someone who was once alive for God but lost that zeal along the way. It can so easily happen! We start off with excitement for God, but then life takes its course. Obligations and disappointments quench much of the spiritual life we once had. Some become cynical or even lose their faith altogether.

It's true that youthful zeal can be misdirected or unsustainable, but even so, don't we miss the passion, the joy, the presence of God, and the reality of the faith we once had? Pray that God will revive those things in you again!

> Yes, Lord, revive me! Restore the
> passion I had for You. Amen.

93

Salvation is near

Surely His salvation is near to those who
fear Him, that glory may dwell in our land.
PSALM 85:9

Take this as a personal promise: surely salvation is near those who fear God. What a wonderful and great assurance, which always remains true. Salvation is near, because God is near!

He is your salvation, not some or other hoped for event, blind luck, or influential person to whom you may be looking. Let's put it this way: For us as Christians help is always near, just around the corner – always imminent! Faith knows that it can happen at any time. That's how faith operates.

It remains expectant, trusting, longing, waiting! Remember, our relationship with God rests on faith. It's our way of living. Live therefore with strong faith, with great expectations! Confess your faith, wait for God in faith, receive what He gives in faith. Do not hesitate or retreat – salvation is near!

Lord, I do believe, but help my unbelief (Mark 9:24)! Amen.

Contractual benefits

> Protect me and save me because You are my God.
> I am Your faithful servant, and I trust You.
> PSALM 86:2 (CEV)

See how David identifies the two persons involved in his petition: (1) "You are my God," and (2) "I am Your faithful servant." These concepts evoke the terminology of the covenant between Israel and God, which in the Old Testament is often formulated as, I will be your God; you will be My people.

David applies the covenant personally, because as an individual he feels part of it. God will be his God! That's why he prays with boldness. He feels he has kept his part of the agreement – he is "faithful" and can therefore appeal to God's part of the agreement, which stipulates that God will provide for him.

Remember, as believers we are part of the exact same covenant. Isn't that wonderful? Commit yourself 100 percent to Him, as He has committed Himself 100 percent to you.

Lord, Your covenant is very important to me.
Help me to keep to my side of it, in Jesus' name! Amen.

95

In the pit

> You have put me in the depths of
> the pit, in the regions dark and deep.
>
> PSALM 88:6

This psalm is probably the darkest in the entire Bible. Heman, David's court singer, describes his condition in detail: "Your wrath lies heavy upon me, and You overwhelm me with all Your waves. ... My eye grows dim through sorrow" (Ps. 88:7-9) – and much more!

Only those who know depression will realize the gravity of what he feels. All color disappears from life: nothing can be enjoyed, nothing is worth the effort. Do you know the condition? Do consult a doctor or a knowledgeable counselor – it will really help!

Can I also add the following: depression is a common condition and well known in the Bible; God knows about you and is with you – whether you feel it or not; and you can work through episodes of depression in a meaningful way. You can learn to manage it with God's help. Talk with God about it!

> When all is darkness, Lord, shine Your light!
> In Your light I will see the Light. Amen.

96

From eternity to eternity

Lord, You have been our dwelling place in
all generations. Before the mountains were
brought forth, or ever You had formed the earth and
the world, from everlasting to everlasting You are God.

PSALM 90:1-2

In the midst of many troubles, Moses feels heartened by the fact that God exists from eternity to eternity. Although the earth and mountains were seen in those times as symbols of absolute immovability, Moses says they are small and insignificant compared to the greatness of God.

Against the awesome backdrop of God's greatness man is even more diminutive, fleeting, and fragile. Remember that God also created time. For Him, our future is as exactly well-known as our past! Still — and this is the wonder of His greatness — God enters into our own time and comes to live our little lives with us.

As we live moment by moment, wondering and deciding, God is with us. When we're worried about the future, though, He is not worried, because He already knows precisely how our future will end: in glory, with Him!

Thank You, Lord, for being
my beginning and my end! Amen.

97

A thousand years

For a thousand years in Your sight are but as yesterday when it is past, or as a watch in the night.

PSALM 90:4

We often think, wrongly so, that God lives in time as we do. No, God exists over time, because He created it. God looks upon yesterday, today, and tomorrow as if they are mere points on a graph.

Moses realizes this when he says in this verse that a thousand years for God is like yesterday: concluded, done, already half-forgotten and unreal. Like a "watch in the night," which is slept through in an instant. Although for us a thousand years is an extremely long time, for God it's a mere moment. On the other hand, God can also change everything in an instant, because a second for Him is like a year to work in.

The lesson is this: Let's not be so concerned about time and about timing, because God isn't! Whatever He does, God is always on time! Just keep on trusting Him.

Eternal God, in Your eyes my life is already concluded in You: finished, accomplished, won! Amen.

Teach us to live

> So teach us to number our days
> that we may get a heart of wisdom.
>
> PSALM 90:12

Remember, Moses saw God's majesty with his own eyes! Therefore, he was deeply under the impression of how small and fragile man really is. He stresses that we only live for seventy or eighty years, and he prays that we will use our years to obtain wisdom.

What he is asking for here is that life itself be our teacher, that life be the course that we follow in order to achieve the goals that God has in mind for us. Live therefore with an open and inquiring mind, eager to grasp whatever you can learn. Develop depth. Above all, don't be afraid to fail, because failure is necessary for learning. We will fail and we must fail! Learn to fail productively, though.

Do not take it too personally. Understand the lessons to be learned and adapt your behavior accordingly. Eventually you will obtain what the Bible calls wisdom – a worthy goal!

*Master, teach me wisdom. Use my life
and teach me how to live. Amen.*

99

Satisfy us

> Satisfy us in the morning with Your steadfast love,
> that we may rejoice and be glad all our days.
>
> PSALM 90:14

Moses states that man is small before his Creator and that his days are few, beset with many challenges. He is praying, therefore, that God will always be with them. Here he specifically asks for God's "steadfast love," for His lovingkindness to "satisfy [them] in the morning."

What beautiful words – read them again – describing our need for God as a hunger to be satisfied! More specifically, our need is for God's steadfast love – His sworn covenant-love, in other words. We merely ask for what God has already promised! Consider this: Will God do what He promised? Most assuredly He will, because He is God! His promises are completely certain – a solid foundation to build upon.

We will experience His steadfast love, no matter what! Like Moses, we can wait upon it "in the morning" – and be satisfied by it. Then, as Moses states, we will rejoice and be glad in it every day!

Lord, satisfy me with Your love as I
wait upon You in the morning. Amen.

My refuge, my fortress

> I will say to the Lord, "My refuge and
> my fortress, my God, in whom I trust."
>
> PSALM 91:2

The unknown poet of these beautiful verses introduces God as the Most High and then as the Almighty. He asserts that the one who finds refuge with that God will surely be safe. In the next verse the mood changes and becomes personal and intimate.

The language becomes that of a personal God and a personal relationship. It's the language of personal faith. It also answers the question: Where do I find the shelter of the Most High, and the shadow of the Almighty?

Well, you will find that refuge in a personal relationship with God. It's in your conversation with Him, in His Word speaking to you; it's in your attention to His voice, in your reaction to His instruction. There you will know that your God is the Highest, the Mighty One. Look for Him there!

*Lord, my need is for more of You in my life,
more relationship – more, Lord! Amen.*

101

Reprogram yourself

A thousand may fall at your side, ten thousand
at your right hand, but it will not come near you.

PSALM 91:7

This psalm is about the fact that God protects us. We needn't fear (Ps. 91:5-6). To not fear is an important but difficult thing to do.

Fear comes naturally! Remember, fear is a basic instinct programmed into us for the sake of our survival. Fear keeps us from danger, because arrows and pestilences can hurt us. However, fruitless and unnecessary fear is counterproductive. We therefore need to work productively with our fear, and we do it through faith.

If we reprogram ourselves with truths such as in this psalm, we take away fear's sting because fear responds to a perceived threat. See it like this: When this psalmist confirms that he will not fear, he is reprogramming his soul with God's truths. Yes, let the truth about God's protection take hold of your soul! As it sinks into your spirit and changes who you are, your fear will decrease – your faith will increase!

Thank You, Lord, that I need not fear.
Teach me not to fear! Amen.

The supernatural

> For He will command His angels concerning you to guard you in all your ways. On their hands they will bear you up, lest you strike your foot against a stone.
>
> PSALM 91:11-12

We don't just live this natural life. According to Scripture, the supernatural is also part of our lives. It must be, because we believe in a supernatural God who intervenes on this earth and in this life!

In this verse we again encounter God's angels, who are extensively mentioned in the Old and New Testaments. The angels are appointed to guard over us, amongst other duties, for which we can be very grateful. In just the next verse we encounter other supernatural beings, too, referred to as lions, adders, and serpents to be trampled underfoot.

In the New Testament these symbols clearly refer to the Evil One and his spirits. How do we deal with him? Well, we keep him under our feet as an act of faith. We rule over him in Jesus' name!

Lord God, help me to live wisely. Command Your angels over me, deliver me from evil! Amen.

103

Forget their prosperity

> Though the wicked sprout and spread like grass, they will be pulled up by their roots.
>
> PSALM 92:7 (CEV)

The psalmist is singing a beautiful song about God's greatness. In this verse he's struggling with the fact that godless people often prosper but feels vindicated by the conclusion that God will wipe them out.

We already dealt with the topic of the success of the godless, so let's add here just the following: forget the godless and forget their prosperity. There will always be those who have more than us. Many will have newer cars or bigger houses. If we fixate on that, we will always feel inferior. Leave them to God, who will judge all people fairly. Let's rather focus on those who have less than us.

There are so many in whose eyes we are the fortunate, the ones having abundance and prosperity. Be grateful for what you have, therefore – and be willing to share with those who struggle. Do you see how your perspective changes the whole matter?

Thank You, Lord, for my prosperity! Make me generous with what I have received. Amen.

Draw deeply

> They will be like trees that stay healthy
> and fruitful, even when they are old.
>
> PSALM 92:14 (CEV)

The righteous can expect God's blessing. It's always true, because God always blesses! To be blessed is our default position in God. In the Old Testament, God's blessing was seen in things like ample rain, good harvests, many children, material wealth, the respect of the community, good health, and a long life.

To see your grandchildren and great-grandchildren was also seen as a great blessing. Here the psalmist says the righteous will keep their vigor and productivity in their old age. It's true that we receive these blessings in varying amounts because we live in an imperfect world, but let's have more faith.

Ask God for these blessings, receive them by faith, and live them! May God bless and reward your expectant heart.

> Father, You are a good God. I so want to draw
> deeply from Your fountain of blessing. Amen.

105

High above

> The floods have lifted up, O Lord, the floods have
> lifted up their voice; the floods lift up their roaring.
> Mightier than the thunders of many waters, mightier
> than the waves of the sea, the Lord on high is mighty!
>
> PSALM 93:3-4

This short psalm has an interesting structure. It starts and ends with the indestructibility of the earth and the security of God on His throne. Then, in the middle we find these verses about the raging and thundering waters.

Remember that the dark and restless waters were seen in the Bible as a symbol of peril and chaos. What does it all mean? Well, there will be difficulties in life, even onslaughts. When difficulties happen they take center stage of our attention.

Everything starts to revolve around the problem. However, if we look away for a bit, if we just look around – and up – we'll see God's might encompassing all our weaknesses, His throne towering high, high above our problems. Listen! You are actually completely safe.

*Thank You, Lord, for being with me,
for being in full control! Amen.*

Do you see it?

> In His hand are the depths of the earth; the heights
> of the mountains are His also. The sea is His,
> for He made it, and His hands formed the dry land.
>
> PSALM 95:4-5

What a beautiful psalm of praise! The reader is called upon to worship the Creator, who made everything good. The Bible teaches us that all men can see God's hand in nature. Do you see it?

Learn to intensely enjoy and appreciate the beauty of the environment around you: the majesty of snow-tipped mountains, the lushness of dark forests, a babbling brook in a deep valley. These are all God's works! Recognize God in the mild and golden autumn days, in sweet spring evenings laden with fragrances and colors.

Exclaim, then, with the poet, "God is great!" Have you lost God somewhere along the way? Then reorient yourself in nature. Get outside, especially early in the morning. Take in the fresh air, and look around. The Creator who made everything is working all things for good in your life.

*My God, when I think of all You
have made, my soul sings! Amen!*

107

Great is the Lord

For great is the Lord, and greatly to be praised;
He is to be feared above all gods.

PSALM 96:4

This psalm is from the beginning to end one great call to praise. The psalmist says God must be praised because He's great above all gods. We usually think that God must be praised for the blessings He bestows on us, but above all God must be praised for who God is.

Praise befits Him, for He is God! Remember that God does not need our praise. He is not so petty as to demand validation from men – or otherwise He'll get angry! Definitely not. No, we need praise! Praise brings *us* into the right relationship with Him.

It confirms Him as God and us as – well, not God. It teaches us to live with faith, because when we praise we confess – in good and bad times – that we have a great God in our lives. Learn to praise as a spiritual discipline!

*Lord, I praise You because You're God.
Be, then, God in my life! Amen.*

Only God can judge ...

> For He comes, for He comes to judge the earth.
> He will judge the world in righteousness,
> and the peoples in His faithfulness.
>
> PSALM 96:13

It's interesting how the people of the Old Testament expected God to come to earth and set things right. Believers always expect God's coming – and God is coming!

God *will* come to judge, because God is the Judge. Judging is God's business, although we so eagerly want to judge as well! Yet, Scripture is clear that judgment – and condemnation – belongs to God alone. The reason is that only He has all the information about a person's heart. We only have certain information and a particular perspective, which means that our judgment can never be truly comprehensive or fair.

Let's just refrain from condemning people left and right. Especially, let's never write people off, because God never writes them off – He keeps on working in the worst of men. To change hearts and lives is His specialty! Let's rather just treat everyone with love and respect.

*Lord, help me not to judge or condemn.
Help me to love! Amen.*

109

Emotions can be moved

Make a joyful noise to the Lord, all the earth;
break forth into joyous song and sing praises!

PSALM 98:4

Can you see that this verse does not contain a friendly request? No, it's a straightforward command that all must praise God with joy and singing! It requires mere obedience.

Perhaps you might say that you don't *feel* like praising, and that it's important to stay true to one's emotions. It's indeed true that we need to be in touch with our emotions and not live a false life, yet Scripture often prescribes certain emotions to us as well. We, for example, have injunctions to love, to not hate, to not be jealous, to not fear or despair, to forgive others – all these are emotions.

Let's put it like this: While we do have genuine feelings and need to acknowledge them, we cannot be controlled by those feelings. They're not in charge of us! We can move, emotionally, to a better place. God will help us – He's in charge!

> Lord, move my emotions to those
> that will glorify You. Amen.

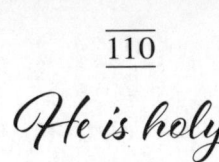

110

He is holy

Exalt the LORD our God;
worship at His footstool! Holy is He!

PSALM 99:5

In this psalm we read three times that God is holy. Holiness is an attribute of God – just think of the seraphim before God's throne who call out day and night, "Holy, holy, holy!" (Isa. 6:3).

Holiness means to be completely separated, and in that sense God is completely different from us: utterly perfect, whole, good – against our own imperfection, brokenness, and sin. What are we to make then of Scripture's injunction that we, mere men, are to become holy? Is that even possible? Let's emphasize this: holiness can never be something we work from our own strength. It's not about trying harder. Holiness is an attribute of God alone and can only be had *from* God alone!

It will happen when we turn our lives more and more onto Him. What the world will then see from us is never our holiness, but always His holiness. Spend more time with God, and holiness will happen by itself!

Lord, as I gaze upon Your holiness, make me holy! Amen.

111

God loves people!

Make a joyful noise to the LORD, all the earth!
PSALM 100:1

This beautiful and well-known psalm forms the end of a cycle in which the whole world is called on to serve God. God wants to be the God of every person! Can we realize how much God loves people?

He enjoys making them in never-ending variations – no two are alike! Just think of the Lapp and Inuit people (Eskimos) of the Northern Arctic, the original Indians of North and South America, the many African peoples, the different European nations, the numerous Arab, Indian, and Chinese people groups, the other inhabitants of the East and of the islands, all the way to the Maori of New Zealand.

Every group and every individual is different. God evidently loves diversity! We are often hesitant about others' differences. We often find our safety in the familiar. If we, however, can learn to love all people as persons loved by God, it will add to God's dream that one day there will be believers gathered around His throne from all tribes, tongues, and nations!

> Lord, give me a love for people
> because You love people! Amen.

112

Standing back

> Know that the LORD, He is God! It is He
> who made us, and we are His; we are
> His people, and the sheep of His pasture.
>
> PSALM 100:3

God who masterly made everything also takes complete ownership of His creation. He made it, and therefore it's His! We ascribe high worth to each person because the Almighty skillfully fashioned them, personally!

Also, each person belongs to Him! Think of God as an artist who feels proud of what He made and remains concerned over His artworks. Isn't it so sad that God's authorship and ownership is so widely denied today? Many would rather attribute our exquisite and intricate universe to an unbelievably small factor of chance than to consider the possibility of an intelligent being behind it all.

For us, though, there was an artist who made everything perfect, and then stood back – as artists do – to declare it "good," magnificent (Gen. 1:31)! Yes, God made you personally. He made you good, and you are His!

Thank You, Lord, for Your beautiful works. Thank You also for making me beautiful in every way! Amen.

113

Something in the heart

> I will sing of steadfast love and justice;
> to You, O Lord, I will make music.
>
> PSALM 101:1

David is singing again! His heart is making him take up his harp. He feels moved to compose a song about how he feels, to play and sing!

Other artists would want to write about their feelings or capture them as a painting, a dance, or a drama. Through the centuries people have produced artworks for the church, knitted jerseys for the children, manned soup kitchens in the winter, or helped repair the church's roof – because they felt something in their hearts! Our questions therefore are: What do you feel in your heart for God? How do you want to express it?

Do you want to sing, to make something, to make a difference, to help somewhere? Be your unique self, and convey your love for God in your unique way. Are you still stuck at the first question? Make it a matter between you and God, and find the answer.

> Lord, I am moved by You in my heart.
> How can I act on it? Amen.

What you focus on

> I will not set before my eyes anything
> that is worthless. I hate the work of those
> who fall away; it shall not cling to me.
>
> PSALM 101:3

David is writing here as the king of Israel. He spells out what kind of a king he wants to be. First he wants a sincere walk with God. Then he wants to be a good and just king. He will not pursue unworthy goals.

Literally, he says he will "not set anything worthless before his eyes," meaning he will not focus on things that are not worthwhile. It reminds us of the fact that we become what we focus on. That on which you spend your time and effort becomes your habit, your lifestyle – it becomes who you are!

Please don't be drawn into unworthy goals, habits, or company – don't let it cling to your soul and define who you're becoming. No, focus on worthy goals! Focus especially on God; make God your goal. Now, that's worthwhile!

> Lord, let my eyes only see what is good and
> worthy. Let my eyes only look at You. Amen.

115

There comes a day

> You will arise and have pity on Zion; it is the time
> to favor her; the appointed time has come.
>
> PSALM 102:13

This psalm is about a person going through a very dark time. His body is ill, he is mentally exhausted, and he feels spiritually worn out and abandoned. Then the mood changes and we suddenly find the language of faith.

"You will arise!" He feels that God's time, "the appointed time," has come. How wonderful that there is such a time! Yes, on a day the current season will be over and the next one will begin. It often happens unexpectedly. Faithfully wait on the next season as you faithfully do what this season asks of you.

Ask yourself questions like these: What is the purpose of this season of my life? How can I work together with God so that the purpose of this season can be accomplished? How can I live in this season so that God will be honored?

> Lord, what is the purpose of this season
> in my life? How should I live in it? Amen.

116

Faith and the future

> The children of Your servants shall dwell secure;
> their offspring shall be established before You.
>
> PSALM 102:28

The psalmist is worried about his country. The people have been captured, Jerusalem has been ravaged, the temple has been torn down. Will there ever be a future in their country again? Then he realizes that God can be trusted. He confesses his belief that their children "shall dwell secure" and serve the God of their fathers. God will see to their children!

Let's take a leaf from his book about our own future. What type of Christians are we when we have no hope? What faith do we demonstrate to the next generation when we tell them there is no future?

It's no faith at all! There is a future for us, and there is a future for our children. In fact, there is a good and blessed future, because God is in that future! He will look after us and after our children. Tell them that!

> Father, forgive me when I speak without faith.
> I do believe in the future You have for us! Amen.

117

Slow to anger

> The LORD is merciful and gracious, slow to
> anger and abounding in steadfast love.
>
> PSALM 103:8

How beautiful is this description of the Lord! The portrayal of God as "slow to anger" goes against a popular but false notion that God is essentially displeased with man, even wrathful, ready to punish the slightest transgression.

On the contrary! The same Old Testament from which such views are deduced often testifies of God's goodness and grace, of His "lovingkindness" that is "new every morning" (Lam. 3:22-23). God's kindness and love are much greater than His wrath! On the other hand, though, we should not miss the fact that God does indeed get angry! What angers God?

We read in the Word that injustice angers God (Prov. 11:1), as does hatred and rebellion – especially after a time, because God is "slow to anger." There comes a point, though, when God says enough, when He demands obedience, justice, goodness, righteousness. And that's a good thing!

Lord, thank You for Your patience and grace!
Help me to stay obedient to Your will. Amen.

God is a dad

As a father shows compassion to his children,
so the Lord shows compassion to those who fear Him.

PSALM 103:13

---

*I*n Scripture God is described by many images, comparisons, and metaphors. For example, God is like a king, a judge, a shepherd, a lion, and a rock. Every image highlights an aspect of God.

The image that says the most about God, however, is that of God as a father. In fact, throughout the New Testament, God is called "the Father". What does a father do? Well, a father brings forth his children, to start with, and then protects and nurtures them. A father educates his children and demonstrates how to live life by his example.

A father allows his children to stand on their own two feet but remains involved and near, ready to catch them when they should fall. Such a father is God! Our lesson is this: the heavenly Father can be fully trusted, because He is the best dad there is!

*Thank You, Abba Father, that I can trust You
fully in every aspect of my life! Amen.*

119

Raw materials

> For He knows our frame; He remembers that we are dust.
> PSALM 103:14

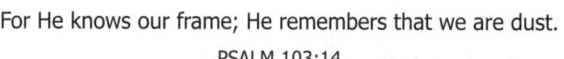

God knows us so well. He knows our failings and our frailty. He "remembers" that we are "dust" – because it was He who made us from dust in the first place! Yes, physically we're made from the ordinary raw materials of the earth: oxygen, hydrogen, nitrogen, carbon.

Also in the mix are small amounts of other elements. As chemicals, we are really worth little. We consist of about fifty liters of water, a small bag of charcoal, enough fat for ten bars of soap, a kilo of chalk, enough iron for one nail, phosphorus to cover some matches, and that's it!

As a human being, though – a living person with needs, fears, and dreams – as a unique creation, each individual is immeasurably valuable to God. Yes, the Creator deeply loves us – whom He made so artfully – and desires a relationship with us. It's exactly our frailty and dependency that draws Him to us. Say yes to His love!

It's wonderful, Father, that You consider a struggling and needy person like me as precious. Amen.

Bloom where you grow

> As for man, his days are like grass; he flourishes
> like a flower of the field; for the wind passes over
> it, and it is gone, and its place knows it no more.
>
> PSALM 103:15-6

Man's life is like a flower that opens, blooms for a little while, withers, and falls off. Does such a flower have any purpose?

Absolutely! That plant grabs at its one chance to live, to survive! It will bloom if it only can – even on the rocks. If it then dies off and centuries roll by and no one ever knew that such a plant existed, what does it matter? It did what it was made to do. It succeeded!

Similarly, you and I received a divine task to live. Accept therefore your assignment, and live with purpose, with meaning, with everything in you! That is God's will. Don't let the promise of eternity detract you from first living this life fully. Bloom where you grow!

Lord, help me to find Your will in these short years of my life. Fulfill my purpose. Amen.

121

Seek God's face

Seek the Lord, and His strength: seek His face evermore.

PSALM 105:4 (KJV)

In this verse the righteous are called upon to seek God's presence – or literally, God's "face." It makes us think of the priestly blessing, in which God promises to lift up His face upon us: "The Lord make His face to shine upon you and be gracious to you; the Lord lift up His countenance upon you and give you peace" (Num. 6:25-26).

Of course, God's face is a symbol of God Himself, of His presence. What we deduce, however, from these two occurrences is that there are two sides to God's blessing: *He* promises to shine His face over us, but *we* need to seek His face, continually. Yes, we cannot just expect or wait for God's blessing.

We must seek it out, receive it, live in it – intentionally! How do we receive it? Well, it's received in God's presence, in relationship with Him! In His presence we'll find enough blessing to take us through the day.

> Lord, Your presence in my life is
> the biggest blessing I know! Amen.

Eternal relationship

> He remembers His covenant forever, the word
> that He commanded, for a thousand generations.
> PSALM 105:8

The psalmist refers us to history as motivation to serve God full out. He points us to the covenant between God and Abraham and how it extended to Isaac, Jacob, Joseph, Moses, and the whole of Israel.

Here he underlines especially that the covenant was established by God "forever … for a thousand generations." Remember, as Christians we are part of that same covenant! God assumes full responsibility for the relationship but also requires of us certain things. He assures us that this relationship is crucial for us and will bless us with many benefits.

Please place a very high value on God's life-giving relationship with you! I once met a man who wore a ring with a cross engraved on its stone. He said it was to remind him that he is covenanted with God. That's so beautiful!

*Lord, Your covenant with me is all-important –
it keeps me alive spiritually. Thank You! Amen.*

123

The crisis has a purpose

> When He summoned a famine on the land
> and broke all supply of bread, He had sent a man
> ahead of them, Joseph, who was sold as a slave.
>
> PSALM 105:16-17

Joseph took food to his brothers in the field, but they seized him and sold him to travelling merchants. Afterward they told their father, Jacob, a lie about a wild animal killing his son.

The news devastated poor Jacob! Where was God in this situation? Why didn't He stop the atrocious deed? Why did a righteous man have to suffer? That's how we would have reacted, wouldn't we? From God's perspective everything happened as it should, though.

A great famine was coming, so God sent Joseph to guarantee the survival of His people. For many years this purpose was not clear, but afterward it all fell into place. Let's trust God more! Let's accept that God is at work. Let's accept that the crisis has a purpose – whether the purpose is known to us now is less important.

> Lord, I do not understand what is happening,
> but I trust that You are in control! Amen.

In the desert?

> They asked, and He brought quail,
> and gave them bread from heaven in abundance.
> He opened the rock, and water gushed out;
> it flowed through the desert like a river.
>
> PSALM 105:40-41

The unknown psalmist is teaching us lessons from Israel's trek through the desert. When the sun burned hot, God was a cloud over them. When they were hungry, He gave them quails and manna.

These things were not always available, but when they were needed, they were there. We also experience the desert times in our lives, but difficulties focus us back to our priorities – and they bring us back to God! If our eyes are open to it, we will see God's grace operating even then. There will be small mercies, the right word at the right time, sustenance needed for another day, or a much needed rest.

Do you notice what God is doing? He is helping you through! Soon the landscape will change – life will be green and lush again, there will be still waters. Desert times pass!

Thank You, Lord, for small mercies, and thank You for Your grace, carrying me through! Amen.

125

Remember me

> Remember me, O LORD, when You show favor
> to Your people; help me when You save them.
> PSALM 106:4

The psalmist is thinking of God's love for His people and is asking here for that love to also extend to him. He wants to be included on the day of salvation! Although God loves all people, not all people are saved (John 1:11-13).

God's unstoppable will includes my own free will. His immeasurable love asks to be loved back; His great invitation expects an unreserved "yes". God will not force or push anyone. He wants to work with our complete and whole-hearted acceptance. You and I must *want* it, *ask* for it, and *take* it in faith.

God's promise is, however, that any honest yearning after Him will surely find Him! God is not making it difficult. No, He wants you to come. He is ready and waiting for you. Just say the words like those of the psalmist: "Remember me, Lord, include me in Your salvation!"

Yes, Lord, I come! I so need You in my life. Amen.

It's them, it's us, it's me

> Both we and our fathers have sinned; we have committed iniquity; we have done wickedness.
>
> PSALM 106:6

Take note how the psalmist is identifying with the sins of his people. He speaks on behalf of all of Israel when he says: "We have sinned. We have done wrong."

What a mature way of praying! Mature prayer is praying for others' problems. We can pray even more maturely by praying on behalf of others – not with the notion that we are spiritual and they are not (and that we do what they should have done), but with the realization that their sin is our sin. When we realize that they are us – our family, our congregation, our leaders, our country, our common humanity – then we get to the point of true humility.

At that point we know that we are basically the same sinful human beings saved purely by grace, and we plead for God's mercy toward all of us. Now that is true intercession!

> Lord, I want to intercede for others.
> We have done wrong, Lord! Amen.

Steer the boat!

> He made the storm be still, and the waves of the sea
> were hushed. ... He brought them to their desired haven.
>
> PSALM 107:29-30

Just as God saved His people from captivity, He saves many people from all kinds of danger. The psalmist is describing here how God saved sailors from a storm on the sea.

They called unto God and the waves were hushed. Let's apply these images in a very practical way. You and I are on a voyage as well. We are travelling to the harbor of our destination, the purpose for which our souls were created. It is the place where everything that God put in us will bear fruit – where we will experience deep satisfaction and meaning.

Life's storms, however, can keep us from reaching that purpose. At times our whole life is just about weathering the storms – so much so that we forget about the destination altogether! Keep your eyes on the goal, and keep on pushing toward your purpose. With God you can become what you must become!

Lord, bring me to my life's destination! Amen.

Learn to walk

> He turns rivers into a desert, springs of water
> into thirsty ground. He turns a desert into pools
> of water, a parched land into springs of water.
> PSALM 107:33, 35

Can you see the turnabout in these verses? God turns rivers into a desert, and then desert into rivers. He can do it either way depending on His plan or what is needed.

With God, things often happen differently. Sometimes He doesn't provide streams in the desert, or takes away the stream and creates a desert. Remember, He is not just the Lamb, He is also the Lion; He is not just our Father, He is also our Judge. We evidently cannot predict God simplistically or put Him in the box of our small understanding.

But now, if God does what He wants (He does, you know), how shall we live? Well, let's not predict too much of what God will do. Let's remain open to His loving decisions. Let's trust Him completely, because He is trustworthy! Let's learn to walk with God – on a day-by-day basis.

Lord, teach me to daily walk with You. Amen.

129

The king who takes control

The Lord says to my Lord: "Sit at My right hand,
until I make Your enemies Your footstool."

PSALM 110:1

This psalm is about the king of Israel, who was appointed by God to rule. To the extent that the king stays at God's "right hand" he would remain God's "right hand man."

Even in the New Testament this psalm is understood Messianically, in other words as referring to Christ. Wasn't He called the "king of the Jews"? Indeed, we believe that Jesus conquered every enemy through His cross and resurrection and now sits at the right hand of the Father. Let's accept Jesus' kingship as a biblical, but also very personal, fact. He wants to be king of my life!

We often want to accept Christ as Savior, but the King isn't satisfied to just act as an insurance policy in our lives. Oh no, when King Jesus moves in, He wants to take over. He wants full control! Let's not misunderstand. With Christ, it's all or nothing.

Lord, be my Savior, but also be Lord of my life! Amen.

130

God's deeds

Full of splendor and majesty is His work, and His righteousness endures forever. He has caused His wondrous works to be remembered; the Lord is gracious and merciful.

PSALM 111:3-4

---

*I*n these verses the deeds of the Lord are praised. It's interesting that we can group God's deeds here as follows:

- God's *great* deeds are "full of splendor and majesty." They are the things that change everything: when your life is spared, when you find a soulmate, when your children are born, when doors open that change your life's direction. These things make you want to praise God!
- God's *small* deeds are those in which His grace and mercy are shown. They're less conspicuous, but just as wonderful. They are the things that make you realize that God is still faithful, that He's still carrying you, blessing you, providing for you daily. They give you peace.

It's easy to see God in the big things, but He is just as present in the small things: the everyday grace, the silent blessings, the moments of mercy.

Lord, open my eyes and let me see
Your works, great and small! Amen.

True wisdom is with Him

> The fear of the Lord is the beginning
> of wisdom; all those who practice it have a
> good understanding. His praise endures forever!
>
> PSALM 111:10

The Bible stands on the fact that true wisdom originates with God. Nowadays that is not so readily believed. On the contrary, much of contemporary "wisdom" starts off by denying God and deciding that man will find his own way. Knowledge and science have been largely disconnected from God and are now standing on their own feet.

Yes, the ideas and values of popular culture are most often leading people away from God. Consider this, however: Earthly wisdom can only produce knowledge and experience about life. About the purpose of life, it can add little! Therefore, it remains a fact that true wisdom starts with God – with an actual relationship with God, with "the fear of the Lord."

In a relationship with Him we receive His wisdom and insight, His purpose for living, and especially His direction for our lives. Be wise in the Lord!

Lord, teach me how to live! Amen.

Joy in the commandments

> Praise the LORD! Blessed is the man who fears the LORD, who greatly delights in His commandments!
> PSALM 112:1

God does not just want us to obey His commandments. No, He wants us to *want* to obey His commandments. There's a difference! He wants us to find joy in doing His will, to "delight in obeying His commands."

The Jewish faith, therefore, puts an emphasis on the joy of keeping the Torah, thanking God for His law, and following it whole-heartedly and eagerly. It is beautiful, for example, to see the people in Jerusalem spilling out of their homes at the start of the Sabbath to dance with joy in the streets.

As Christians we are not under the law, but also not without the law. The law teaches us God's will, and the Holy Spirit empowers us to grow in God's will freely and joyfully. When we find it heavy to serve God, we are misunderstanding the gospel: serving God is not a burden, it's a pleasure! The gospel is good news. It's liberty!

Lord, it's my greatest joy
to serve You – it's wonderful! Amen.

Short life, long influence

> Wealth and riches are in his house,
> and his righteousness endures forever.
>
> PSALM 112:3

The psalmist is saying here that a righteous man's deeds endure forever. Remember, in biblical terms, man's life is fleeting. If this is so, how can we produce something enduring? We can!

Take note:

- The Lord said we should store up treasures in heaven (Matt. 6:20). Invest therefore in your relationship with God, in His kingdom, in the things that have eternal value.
- You can raise up generations for God on earth. Start with your own children. Build up their faith, instill the kingdom of God in their lives! Then they will be able to pass that on to even the next generation.
- You cannot take anything with you into eternity, except for people. So, take along your children by way of speaking – and your friends, your family! Pray for them and let your life and words testify of God so that they will want to serve Him as well.

Make the decision that your life will have enduring value!

Lord, do Your work in me and through me! Amen.

Do right, be righteous

It is well with the man who deals generously
and lends; who conducts his affairs with justice.
PSALM 112:5

Righteousness is a fundamental requirement of believers, and it should therefore be our honor to live rightly toward God and others: to be God-fearing, to be honest, to be just and fair, to be law-abiding, to speak what is right.

You cannot proclaim to be a Christian, but then not be trustworthy in your deeds or words, unfair, or otherwise unbecoming as a child of God. That's embarrassing to our faith and to God! No, let's live openly and transparently. Let's speak the truth even if it's to our detriment.

Let's not exaggerate or slant what happened – just say exactly and plainly how things were, or are. Let's guard our integrity and good name, because we're children of the Almighty. Remember, He only stands with what is right and true, never with what is wrong or deceitful.

*Lord, I want to stand with You –
by standing with what is right and true! Amen.*

135

Live unfettered

> He has distributed freely; he has
> given to the poor; his righteousness
> endures forever; his horn is exalted in honor.
>
> PSALM 112:9

Here the psalmist asserts that a righteous person is a generous giver. While Jesus said it's more blessed to give than to receive (Acts 20:35), many Christians believe the purpose of their walk with God is to receive blessings.

We even try to claim or obtain such blessings by a variety of spiritual techniques. Yet, the purpose of our faith is to be a blessing! It's our sinful nature that only wants to receive, yet the Spirit helps us to give. Isn't the whole spiritual life an exercise in giving? We give our hearts and lives to God, we give up our own concerns for His, we give love, we give forgiveness, and we give our service!

It's only in the giving that we receive; it's in blessing others that we are blessed ourselves. It's in loving that we find love! Give generously, share freely! That's the way to live.

Lord, teach me to give. I have more than enough! Amen.

136

Sing the song of all creation

> From the rising of the sun to its setting,
> the name of the Lord is to be praised!
>
> PSALM 113:3

What a beautiful verse! The ancients believed that the heavens were like a tremendous dome that was placed over the earth, blue by day and black by night. Underneath this firmament the sun, moon, and stars went about their courses.

The sun coming up in the east and setting in the west circumscribed the whole of creation – and all are called here to praise God! Our contemporary view of east and west still includes all that exists. Take note that all of creation is already praising the Creator. The forces of evil that exist and the effects of man's sin, of course, produce false notes in the otherwise beautiful symphony.

But Jesus is coming, and all will be made right! Let's turn to the Creator, and let's do what we're called to do – honor our Maker!

Beautiful Creator, I want to praise
You the whole day through! Amen.

137

You are worthy

> He raises the poor from the dust and lifts the
> needy from the ash heap, to make them sit with
> princes, with the princes of His people.
>
> PSALM 113:7-8

This psalm testifies about God's greatness. Here we see how God "raises" the poor and needy right across the social spectrum! Those who are sitting in the dust or on the ash heap will eventually sit down with princes at their banquet.

The reference here is to people who were shoved to the margins of society, who were thrown away. Dust and ashes were symbols of sorrow and loss. The reference could also be to those who were sad, who removed themselves from society to mourn. Whatever the case may be, the psalmist assures us that God joins those who suffer and those in sorrow. He sits down with them, where they are, and restores their dignity.

Have you been sidelined in life? Have you suffered loss? Do you feel useless or worthless? Jesus is with you! Jesus is there and things will change!

Lord Jesus, thank You that You're with me today! Amen.

Break the rock

> Tremble, O earth, at the presence of the Lord, at the
> presence of the God of Jacob, who turns the rock
> into a pool of water, the flint into a spring of water.
> PSALM 114:7-8

The psalmist is referring us to Israel's trek from Egypt to Canaan. In the desert when they had no water, Moses struck a rock and enough water streamed out for all. Yes, God turned hard rock into flowing, life-giving water. God can also do that to hardened hearts!

Some people are hard-hearted because they were hurt in the past. Others, though, were brought up to not show emotion. Some have ended up cold and cynical. The Lord, however, can break open such a heart! In fact, the promise of the new covenant is that hearts of stone will become hearts of flesh.

The Holy Spirit *can* flow from even the hardest heart to quench, heal, refresh, and create new life. Yes, it can happen! Keep on praying for hard hearts!

> Lord, I first pray for myself, because I, too,
> find hardness and cynicism in my
> own heart. Break my heart, Lord! Amen.

139

Give away your glory

Not to us, O Lord, not to us, but to Your name give glory,
for the sake of Your steadfast love and Your faithfulness!

PSALM 115:1

We all like to receive attention and honor, to be acknowledged and thanked – to feel that we are important! However, it's not good for the soul to receive too much honor and glory. Our ego cannot handle it and quickly feels overly important.

We forget that it was grace that brought us to this place! "Not to us," says the Word here, "but to Your name" glory should be given. If we are praised, we may sincerely accept it, by all means – it's natural and important. Yes, show your gratitude, but also add (where appropriate) that God is to be thanked. Give as much honor to Him as you can! Then acknowledge the input of others.

Learn to deflect glory. To receive honor doesn't necessarily make you great – to give honor makes you greater!

*Lord, help me to be mature with honor
and acknowledgement. Thank You for the
grace that makes everything possible! Amen.*

You become who you serve

> Those who make them become
> like them; so do all who trust in them.
>
> PSALM 115:8

You become like your god! The psalmist is making this profound statement in regard to the idols of their time. We know the other side of this biblical truth better, that we as Christians become more like Christ.

It's a general truth, though, that we'll transform into the image of whatever god we worship. Those who bow to mammon can only talk about money.

Those who worship status always brag about their success. Those who worship their bodies pose relentlessly before the mirror.

Yes, our idols change us – they change our thinking and behavior. They make us ugly, selfish, obsessive, and anxious. Idols never liberate us! Of course there is nothing wrong with money as such or with getting ahead or with healthy living. Of course not. But when these things become our driving force, our overriding purpose, we must break their bonds in Jesus' name!

Lord Jesus, help me to serve You alone.
Make me more like You! Amen.

141

Blessing, blessing, blessing

> The LORD has remembered us; He will bless us;
> He will bless the house of Israel; He will bless
> the house of Aaron; He will bless those who
> fear the LORD, both the small and the great.
>
> PSALM 115:12-13

In this psalm the people and the priests are called on to trust God. Then the Lord remembered them! He thought of them, and He blessed them!

Those who serve God are really more blessed than any unbeliever can be. Take note that we said "more blessed," not necessarily richer or healthier. These things can be blessings (or not), but the concept of blessing is actually defined a bit differently.

Blessing is experiencing God's favor over your life. It's the privilege of living with God – in the ups and downs! It is to know that God is with you, that you're forever safe, that your purpose is clear. Blessing is to have the peace that surpasses understanding (Phil. 4:7). Those who do not live with God can never have this!

Lord, I receive Your blessing and I thank You for it. Amen.

The burden has lifted

Gracious is the LORD, and righteous; our God
is merciful. The LORD preserves the simple;
when I was brought low, He saved me.
PSALM 116:5-6

Our unknown psalmist tells us how anxious and desperate he was when he called unto God for help. Then these beautiful verses follow about God's help and care. God saved him! Scripture instructs that we shouldn't worry, but pray (Phil. 4:6-7).

Perhaps we should say it like this: *Whenever* you have worries, you can cast them – all your burdens – onto the Lord (1 Pet. 5:7). Then the peace of God will settle over you. Take note, however, that this often entails a process. It takes time for us to experience that peace that surpasses understanding. Therefore, we shouldn't just pray about something and then leave it.

No, we should pray on, push through, until we experience the peace that we need, *until* the burden has lifted and we feel we can leave the matter with God. Yes, sometimes peace takes time – yes, often prayer is a real struggle. Carry on praying!

Lord, I pray for Your peace in my heart today. Amen.

143

Confused and disappointed

> I believed, even when I spoke: "I am greatly afflicted;"
> I said in my alarm, "All mankind are liars."
>
> PSALM 116:10-11

The writer of this psalm went through deep waters. The worst was when he realized that in his greatest need he could depend on no one. He stood alone!

Remember, he is not stating a general truth about humankind here. He is describing a painful, personal experience. There are indeed dependable and loving people around us, but in our confusion and distress we often cannot see them. It is really bad for us when we get disappointed again and again and later feel that no one really cares, that everyone is just concerned with their *own* welfare.

Still, if we put our faith in God – as the psalmist did – He will take us through the affliction and then, when our minds are clearer, we will realize that there were good and kind people all along, that our conclusions were hasty. May God help you, and may you find the support you need!

*Lord, I am in need. I need people
to help me through this! Amen.*

144

Precious is your death

Precious in the sight of the Lord is the death of His saints.

PSALM 116:15

The idea here is not to glorify death as something valuable to God. On the contrary, it focuses on the fact that life is so valuable that God is greatly involved when it comes to an end. It has to do with the question of God's involvement in suffering and death. Does He care? Is He near? Why does He allow innocent people to suffer?

We first must remember that suffering and death were never revoked by God. They remain a part of life because of the brokenness that sin produced.

Even Christ had to suffer and die! Only in the next world will there be no death. What the Word emphasizes here, though, is that God remains deeply *involved* with us, that He deeply *cares* wherever there is suffering, pain, and loss. In fact, at our death God will be nearer to us than at any other time. He will meet us right there!

*Lord, thank You that You are
intensely concerned with my life. Amen.*

145

That's who you are!

> Oh give thanks to the LORD, for He is good;
> for His steadfast love endures forever!
>
> PSALM 118:1

This specific pronouncement of praise is found in many psalms. What does it mean, though?

Well, these words are merely the Old Testament version of the New Testament declaration that God is love. It's a definition and description of God's character. God is good, and God's love is endless. That's who God is! Everything God does emanates from His goodness – even His justice, wrath, and punishment are part of His love! Now consider this: God is defined as love, but love cannot hang in the air. Love needs an object.

You have to love something or someone. Isn't that so? What, then, is the object of God's love? Well, among other things we are the objects of God's love – He loves us! That brings us to our identities as humans: we are the beloved of God. Who are you? You are God's beloved – that's who you are!

Thank You, loving Father, that I am the object of Your endless love. I love You also! Amen.

God looks at you

> The stone that the builders rejected
> has become the cornerstone. This is the
> Lord's doing; it is marvelous in our eyes.
>
> PSALM 118:22-23

Jesus was rejected by men, but chosen by God as the foundation on which to build His kingdom. The lesson is that God looks at things differently. That which is wise in the eyes of men may be foolish in the eyes of God – or vice versa. Who we see as weak may be seen by God as a useful instrument to work through. God often takes the least or the humblest to surpass the most important.

So, do you feel as if you don't add much value? Are you at the bottom of the list? Do good things pass you by? Well, blessed are you! God looks at you differently. He *will* use you – and He *will* raise you up in His time!

Lord, thank You that I do not have to compare myself to anyone. You will use me just as I am! Amen.

147

Blessed are you

> Blessed is he who comes in the name of the Lord!
> We bless you from the house of the Lord.
>
> PSALM 118:26

*I*n the original context these words were especially directed to the king who, on the day of the feast, led the procession into the temple, but it also included all who followed. In the New Testament the words are applied to Christ, but also to us, following Him into God's sanctuary.

These images make our thoughts wander off to the day that we'll finally enter God's presence. On our eternal arrival into God's abode, a wonderful welcome will await us. A choir will sing a song like this one, and the Church that's already with God will rejoice over yet another believer making it safely home! Jesus will be there with open arms, awaiting us with love in His eyes.

Yes, we know we're speculating. But still, to enter God's presence is always wonderful, and on that day it will surpass everything we have ever known! Blessed are you, overcomer in Christ!

> Lord, thank You for these words
> of grace. They bless me! Amen.

You are blessed!

> Blessed are those whose way is blameless,
> who walk in the law of the Lord!
> PSALM 119:1

This longest psalm in the Bible – 176 verses – is about the Word of God. Take note of the simple message of the Bible concerning obedience: obedience leads to God blessing, while disobedience forfeits God's blessing! This is a fundamental truth that we should accept and live by.

The blessed life is a life with God, a life in His will. Such a life does not guarantee that you won't have bad times, but the blessing is that we can go through those times with God.

That makes quite a difference, because God adds meaning, peace, and victory to all of our seasons. It's always blessed to live with God, good times or bad! Do you need to return to the blessed life?

Lord, Your Word is the truth.
Help me to walk in that truth. Amen.

149

More than riches

> In the way of Your testimonies I delight
> as much as in all riches. I will delight in
> Your statutes; I will not forget Your word.
> PSALM 119:14, 16

Without the Word, we would never know God's will for us. Still, the Lord does not just want us to follow His prescripts because it's *His* will for us or in order to receive the blessing it brings.

No! He wants us to follow them because it has become our will, because we want to, because it delights us, as the psalmist says here. He says following God's decrees brings more pleasure than all the riches in the world! Living with God brings joy and liberty. It's not a burden!

Forget all ideas about a heavy religion or difficult spiritual duties – that is not the biblical emphasis. Ask God to change your heart and start to enjoy serving Him! True joy does not come from riches; it comes from a life in God's will. Break away to that joy!

Lord, You are my greatest joy. Serving You makes my life meaningful, colorful, and rich. Amen.

150

Open my eyes

Open my eyes, that I may behold
wondrous things out of Your law.

PSALM 119:18

We can read Scripture without having it touch our lives. Sometimes the words just roll before our eyes without going into our hearts at all. Our physical eyes may be open, but our spiritual eyes are definitely not!

The Bible often alludes to the fact that we are – spiritually speaking – blind. We carry on without paying attention to God in our lives. We must *wake up*, open our eyes, focus! Then we will perceive God all around us! If we want to "behold wondrous things" from God's Word, our eyes must be opened.

Do the following: Read less, but with more attention. Read audibly, slowly, and intensely. Read with the question: Lord, what do You want to convey to me today? Go back to the phrases that stood out for you. Think about them. Then in faith take a lesson from them into your day.

Lord, open my eyes! I do not just want to read the Bible –
I want to read Your Word for me in the Bible. Amen.

151

Sweeter than honey

How sweet are Your words to my taste,
sweeter than honey to my mouth!

PSALM 119:103

In times gone by, sweet things were scarce and considered a luxury. Special events were therefore always celebrated with treats like dates, sweet fruits, or honey. In this verse the psalmist compares the Word of God to honey.

It's a well-known comparison, but take specific note today of the last three words here: "to my mouth." Honey is only sweet when tasted, when in the mouth, isn't that so? In the same way, the Word of God's goodness is not found between your Bible's leather-bound covers but in your mouth: when it is read, repeated, memorized, prayed, sung, recited, preached, confessed – when it is used!

Make the Word part of your everyday life. Repeat its truths, listen to its psalms, learn its verses, pray about its teachings, and live out its instructions. As you ingest the Word, as it becomes part of you, its sweetness will permeate your day – your whole life!

Lord, thank You for these sweet words.
May Your Word fill my words and actions to Your glory. Amen.

152

Light on the path

Your word is a lamp to my feet and a light to my path.
PSALM 119:105

Life is a journey. Life's road twists away into a dark and unknown future, but we have no choice but to take it. We must walk it not knowing what the next turn will bring!

The road can surprise us with unexpected bends or stops. At other times the way can become so dark that we cannot even see the next step. It's then that we need a light to guide us. Our psalmist assures us that God's Word is the light we need for life's journey!

His Word will cast light on the road and on our purpose and goal and will guide our actions and decisions. With God's Word, we'll find our way again! Remember that we do not walk life's path alone, although we might think so. Oh no, we have a guide, the Holy Spirit. It is He who whispers God's Word in our ear, shining its light, making sure that we reach the goal!

Holy Spirit, shed Your Light on my path! Amen.

153

Mornings remain superb

I rise before dawn and cry for help; I hope in Your words.
PSALM 119:147

We have said that the Bible does not give specific instructions on how or when a personal quiet time should be taken. We have the examples of many biblical or historical faith heroes, though, and our own personal experience to guide us into a spiritual rhythm, a personal walk with God.

Perhaps you have time over lunch for God's Word or on Wednesday afternoons – perhaps over the weekends, when it's quiet? Mornings remain superb, though, for meeting with God! When you're young, you tend to sleep the mornings away, but with maturity you appreciate the freshness of the dawn more and more.

It's absolutely fantastic to get up early, go outside, and experience the day breaking. Breathe it in! It's even better to share it with God, as our psalmist did. Try it!

Father, thank You for lovely mornings,
and thank You for sharing
those mornings with me. Amen.

154

Constant change

> But You are near, O LORD, and all Your commandments
> are true. Long have I known from Your testimonies
> that You have founded them forever.
> PSALM 119:151-152

In biblical times the old things were the good things. Old traditions and practices were not tampered with because they were the proven ones. Innovations were frowned upon as unnecessary and disruptive.

We, on the other hand, live in a time of constant change. In the last century alone the world has seen two great wars, radically changing values, space exploration, and the development of computers. Information, transport, commerce, and media made us world citizens. Old ways have become obsolete and are being replaced by new ones.

Innovation and adaptation have become essential, but all these many changes can be overwhelming, confusing! They create the need for guidance – for discernment, values, direction. The psalmist assures us, however, that God's will remains the same, that His commandments are "forever." Set your compass to God's will – the one true constant amidst the change!

> Lord, thank You that You're the same
> yesterday, today, and forever. Amen.

155

Come after me

> I am Your servant, but I have wandered away
> like a lost sheep. Please come after me,
> because I have not forgotten Your teachings.
>
> PSALM 119:176 (CEV)

The psalmist sincerely wants insight into God's Word, and he wants to be obedient.

More than that, he rejoices in God's law, he loves God's will, and he calls up the reader to do the same. Then he ends this beautiful psalm with this verse: "I have wandered away like a lost sheep. Please come after me." The psalmist knows human nature so well! He knows that we are prone to wandering off. We so easily lose focus, get sidetracked, become busy.

When that happened to our psalmist, he trusted God to come and look for him. Will God seek out His lost sheep? Of course He will! Jesus said the Good Shepherd will leave the ninety-nine to find the one that's not there. Yes, God will come after you! In fact, He is coming for you at this moment. What a relief!

> Thank You, Lord, for seeking me out,
> for finding me, for bringing me home! Amen.

156

Look up, look there!

> I lift up my eyes to the hills.
> From where does my help come?
>
> PSALM 121:1

The composer of this pilgrim song is on his way to Jerusalem. The "hills" that he's looking up to are probably not the general hills of Judea. When the psalms refer in these contexts to hills, they usually mean Jerusalem's hills, most especially Zion, on which God's temple stood.

It means the pilgrim is looking ahead – to his destination, to the temple, and to *Yahweh*, the Lord from whom his help comes. Yes, the pilgrim is keeping his eyes on his goal, which is God! We are also pilgrims on our way to eternity.

Are you perhaps walking with worries or needs, with longings? Do you need help? Your help comes from Him to whom your journey leads! His Spirit will daily guide you to that destination. Know that you will receive your help, you will reach your goal, and you will be safe, forever! Let these truths strengthen your strides today.

Thank You, Lord, that my help is from You!
Give me the strength for today's journey. Amen.

157

You'll be glad

I was glad when they said to me,
"Let us go to the house of the Lord!"

PSALM 122:1

Three times a year Jewish men had to go to Jerusalem to attend a feast. It must have been a disruption, because it involved a long journey.

David, however, was always glad to go to the "house of the Lord." Today, to go to the "house of the Lord" still entails effort and a sacrifice of time. Some Christians have become disappointed in the church and readily point to its failures. Still, the church remains Christ's body on earth and remains God's plan for the world.

So do not give up on the church! Rather, find your place in the church – a place where you can hear the Word, simply and directly, where you will grow spiritually, and where you can serve. Don't see it as an effort or a sacrifice but as a necessary spiritual discipline. If you make the space in your life to meet God, you can be sure God will show up!

*Lord, help me to become
more involved in Your church. Amen.*

The peace of Jerusalem

> Pray for the peace of Jerusalem! "May they
> be secure who love you! Peace be within
> your walls and security within your towers!"
>
> PSALM 122:6-7

The psalmist is calling on the reader to be just as concerned for Jerusalem as he is himself. He wants us to pray for the "peace of Jerusalem."

Jerusalem has had so little peace in its history. The city has been captured and destroyed so many times during the ages! Jesus wept for Jerusalem, who rejected Him, and prophesied its destruction, which happened shortly after (Mark 13). Today Jerusalem is still a city in conflict. We pray for the peace of Jerusalem.

We pray that God will fulfill His plan for His city. We pray for the people of the city, especially for the thousands of Christians staying there. We pray that they – the church of God in Jerusalem – will truly shine the light of Him who was crucified there.

> Yes, Lord, I do pray for Jerusalem,
> the city You love. Grant them peace! Amen.

159

Wait on His hand

> Behold, as the eyes of servants look to the hand of their master, as the eyes of a maidservant to the hand of her mistress, so our eyes look to the Lord our God, till He has mercy upon us.
>
> PSALM 123:2

We find descriptions from ancient times of formal functions in which servants stood silently at the end of tables, arms folded, eyes fixed on their master who could communicate with them through simple gestures.

Our psalmist puts us in the position of such a servant of God, and our obedience to God should be as complete as the referenced servant to his master.

Yet, we are often so full of our own will and goals that we remain unhappy and frustrated – and of little use to God. If we could only forget ourselves and look up to the Lord, as this psalm says, and wait on His will as our single duty, we would find a much deeper happiness and meaning. We are called to a total surrender – God needs to help us with that!

Lord, help me to totally surrender to You! Amen.

160

Dreams come true

> When the LORD restored the fortunes
> of Zion, we were like those who dream.
>
> PSALM 126:1

A miracle happened when the king of Babylon decided after seventy years that the Jews could return to their land. Without delay the trek back was organized and implemented – but what a disappointment! Their land was barren and destroyed, inhabited by a new and hostile people.

Whatever they built during the day was torn down during the night. They planted, but it didn't rain. They struggled and despaired with their dream collapsed and gone. Yes, sometimes we work at a dream we have, a vision, but it doesn't work out.

Everything goes wrong, and we end up with loss after loss. It's a fact, of course, that not every dream can work out, but for now let's look at the outcome for these Jews. They did resettle their land, they did conquer their challenges, and their dream did come true! Speak to God about that dream of yours – it can still happen.

Giver of Dreams, I have a dream in my heart,
and I want to share it with You. Amen.

161

Sowing and growing

> Those who sow in tears shall reap with
> shouts of joy! He who goes out weeping,
> bearing the seed for sowing, shall come home
> with shouts of joy, bringing his sheaves with him.
>
> PSALM 126:5-6

The Jews returned from exile, but they found that their land was barren, destroyed, and inhabited by a hostile people. Now they're sowing again, but they're sowing in tears – their dream has collapsed.

Still, they're sowing because they had to sow. Do you know what happened? They had a harvest, and every year they had a better harvest. We must sow, because without sowing there can be no reaping. Only sowing can lead to a harvest. Whether you're disheartened or uncertain, you must sow!

Ask God how and when to sow the right seed on the right land. To sow is our share of the deal; to grow the crop is God's share! Faithfully do what you must – even if it is with many tears – and trust God for the outcome.

*Lord, I'm sowing in tears today,
but I'm trusting You for a joyful harvest! Amen.*

Work and blessing

> Unless the LORD builds the house, those who build
> it labor in vain. Unless the LORD watches over
> the city, the watchman stays awake in vain.
>
> PSALM 127:1

Take note that Scripture, as in this verse, is never against work. It's always for hard work, responsible work. Still, work is not everything. The question always must be, where does God fit into all this working? The lesson of this psalm is emphatically the following: If God is not in our work, we're working in vain.

If His blessing is not upon us, all our efforts are hopeless. "It is in vain that you rise up early and go late to rest, eating the bread of anxious toil" (Ps. 127:2). For those whom God loves, He grants His provision even as they sleep.

Let's work then, and let's work hard – but let's also seek God's blessing on what we do, for without that there can be no success. Working is only part of our lives, which wholly belongs to Him!

*Lord, bless my work! Help me to balance it
with what is equally important in my life. Amen.*

163

The circle of blessing

> The Lord bless you from Zion! May you see
> the prosperity of Jerusalem all the days of your life!
>
> PSALM 128:5

In God's beautiful temple on Mount Zion, the priest raises his hands and blesses the people with these words. God promised Moses that if the priests would pray according to His instructions, He would bless the people (Num. 6:22-27).

Yes, receive your blessing in the name of the Lord! Let's add something, though: We cannot just sit and wait for God's blessing. We must actively receive it. That means that we must appropriate it. We must accept it as a truth and then go and live as if we are blessed indeed. To be blessed is an act of faith and part of our obedience.

There is also another way of appropriating our blessing, and that is by blessing others. To bless others activates the principle of sowing and reaping. To be a blessing is to receive blessing, with which we can be even more of a blessing! Get the circle of blessing going!

*Lord, help me to bless wherever I go,
whomever I meet. Amen.*

Wait for the Lord – wait!

> I wait for the LORD, my soul waits, and in His word
> I hope; my soul waits for the Lord more than watchmen
> for the morning, more than watchmen for the morning.
>
> PSALM 130:5-6

To "wait for the Lord" is a well-known concept In Scripture but one that we use less today, perhaps because we don't like to wait. To wait on God is just another way of describing faith. It describes our expectation of God's intervention.

It says that we will *stay* before God with the matter, that we will keep our eyes on Him until He intervenes! In Scripture, this waiting-on-God wasn't an uncertain matter. Oh no, biblical hope is being sure about the outcome but having to wait for it to happen.

It's true that to wait isn't always pleasant, but not everything can happen at once. Sometimes we do have to wait. Wait, then, on the Lord: patiently, faithfully – productively!

Lord, give me the patience and the faith to wait! Amen.

165

Silent in the storm

> Surely I have behaved and quieted myself,
> as a child that is weaned of his mother:
> my soul is even as a weaned child.
>
> PSALM 131:2 (KJV)

*T*his short psalm is about the fact that we cannot always understand God, that we often just need to trust Him. God will be God, and faith means to let God be God in our lives.

Therefore, David says that he has "quieted" his soul before God. He has stopped asking questions. Life's questions remained, of course, because his circumstances remained. Around him the storm still raged, but in him he found a quiet place. He has the peace of God.

Like a weaned child, he doesn't want something from God – he merely wants God! This, of course, is difficult for us to attain in our walk with God, but this is what faith can do: it can bring about the peace that surpasses understanding (Phil. 4:7). This is a full surrender, and this is what we need!

> Lord, I do so want to have the peace
> that surpasses understanding! Amen.

166

How pleasant!

Behold, how good and pleasant it is when
brothers dwell in unity! It is like the precious oil on
the head, running down on the beard, on the beard
of Aaron, running down on the collar of his robes!

PSALM 133:1-2

Yes, how wonderful it is when people can live together in peace! Scripture uses the imagery of the Holy Spirit to describe God's blessing and unction on such relationships.

The description of the psalmist makes us think of the Spirit's anointing in this way: First it transforms our thinking, then it flows down to heal our heart's emotions, and then it gets onto our clothes where it becomes part of our behavior.

Finally, it wets the ground around us as a fragrant testimony of God's presence! To be able to live together peaceably is the result of the Spirit's work in our lives and His fruit, which is borne in our behavior (Gal. 5:22-23). We need to be filled by the Spirit – then our relationships will be wonderful as well!

Lord, fill me with Your Spirit!
Bless us with unity and peace. Amen.

167

Inner sanctuary

> Lift up your hands to the holy place
> and bless the Lord! May the Lord bless you
> from Zion, He who made heaven and earth!
>
> PSALM 134:2-3

In this psalm the servants of God are called upon to come and worship at night, in God's sanctuary. They should go to the temple and pray.

There, after praying, they received the priests' blessing and with this blessing they could proceed on their way. In our literal or figurative night, we can also go into the inner sanctuary of the heart and meet with God. There we can raise our hands and praise Him.

It is difficult to praise God during the dark times of our lives but it's so beneficial for the soul! Praise brings us into God's presence; it brings us into obedience – it brings us into faith. Praise leads to a blessing, because upon meeting us in this way God will also raise His hands and "bless [us] from Zion." Yes, as we raise our hands in praise, those hands receive His blessing.

> Lord, teach me to praise,
> and bless me, Lord. Bless from Zion! Amen.

His purpose

> The LORD will fulfill His purpose for me;
> Your steadfast love, O LORD, endures forever.
> Do not forsake the work of Your hands.
>
> PSALM 138:8

What a beautiful confession! God, who started the good work in you, will also complete it. The Bible is clear that God's future holds *full* completion – yes, *full* and *final* closure of the whole grand drama of His work on earth.

Creation leads to consummation! The humans who were driven from Paradise will be welcomed back in the New Jerusalem. Every man and woman ever created will appear before God to account for their lives, where they will be treated justly and appropriately.

Eventually, every good deed will be rewarded and every misdeed punished. Every cause will lead to its effect so that ultimately no loose ends remain. Then perfect peace will reign – perfect harmony, righteousness, and love! No, God will not forsake the work of His hands. Remember, you and I are still in His hands. He is still busy with us!

Thank You, Lord, that You will bring my life to its perfect purpose, as You promised. Amen.

169

God knows

> O LORD, You have searched me and known me!
> You know when I sit down and when
> I rise up; You discern my thoughts from afar.
>
> PSALM 139:1-2

God knows us better than we know ourselves. His eyes search us and search through us. Even more, He searches our soul and knows our thoughts, our feelings, our motives. Yes, He knows our weaknesses and our sin, our self-centered attitude, our wayward thinking, what we do when no one is watching.

God sees our love of money, honor, and power. He knows our jealousy and how hard we can sometimes be. God sees ahead in our lives and knows precisely what the future holds. God sees us on our deathbed. He knows us! Still – and this is the wonder – God loves us! He loves us passionately; He loves every fiber of our being, every motion of our soul.

He intends the best for us! God makes it abundantly clear that the best life for us is a life with Him, because no one knows us as He does!

Thank You, Lord, for knowing me, and still loving me! Amen.

Your hands on me

> You hem me in, behind and before,
> and lay Your hand upon me.
> **PSALM 139:5**

What a beautiful image: God laying His hands on us! God's hands on us means that He is busy forming us, like a potter who is working His clay to make something beautiful. What are the Potter's hands busy with in your life? What is He forming? Well, He is forming you into the image of Christ or, better, forming Christ in you (Gal. 4:19). It's your best you! In this psalm, though, God's hands are protecting us, keeping us from harm.

What can happen with us with God's hands around us? Well, nothing! Nothing that He does not allow! Can the enemy get to you? Can you suffer loss? Can you lose out in life? Never!

Nowhere in the whole world are you safer than in the hands of God. Become more conscious of God's wonderful, strong, and caring hands on your life. Can you feel it? Relax, then. You're in good hands!

> Lord, thank You for Your big, strong hands
> that protect, comfort, and guide me. Amen.

God's presence

> If I ascend to heaven, You are there!
> If I make my bed in Sheol, You are there!
>
> PSALM 139:8

David says God is everywhere. If he were to fly to the east or go and live in the west, God would be there. "From east to west" is a well-known biblical phrase used to describe God's deeds over the whole earth.

God is also in the whole vertical dimension: He is up in heaven, down on earth, and even in Sheol, where, according to Old Testament thought, the dead resided. He is the God of the living and of the dead. The lesson, though, is this: you cannot go anywhere or do anything where God's hands will not guide you or keep you.

Even amidst your biggest fear, God will be there and, ultimately, and on your last day, God will be right there as well. His hands will safely hold you. Yes, with God on the scene we never need to fear! Have some more faith, will you?

*Thank You, Lord, that You are close to me
every day, every place, in life and in death! Amen.*

So near in the darkness

> If I say, "Surely the darkness shall cover me,
> and the light about me be night," even the darkness
> is not dark to You; the night is bright as the day.
>
> PSALM 139:11-12

We have the perception that God is far away when we experience spiritual or emotional darkness, but that's false. In the dark, we cannot see God, but He can see us and remains as near to us as ever before! Yes, in our season of confusion and questions, in our tears and fears, He is actually right next to us – all the time!

Scripture says that God draws near to those who are despairing or heartbroken. That's how His love works! Our problem, therefore, is not just the darkness but the fact that it hides God from us.

We need to focus more on His presence while in the darkness, because He's there! Put out your hand in faith and touch Him.

*Lord, thank You that I can always
reach out and touch You. Always. Amen.*

173

Shine your light on me

Search me, O God, and know my heart! Try me
and know my thoughts! And see if there be any
grievous way in me, and lead me in the way everlasting!

PSALM 139:23-24

In this psalm David asks God to shine His light right through him — to "search" him and "try" him. He wants God to "know" his thoughts: to discern the good and the bad. He specifically appeals to God to test his heart and see if there is any "grievous way" in him — a term referring to the lure toward idol worship.

Although David never outwardly worshiped idols, he is asking God here to show him even the subtlest of motives in his heart that might detract him from God.

What a wonderful love for God is this! We, on the other hand, would rather try to hide, minimize, or excuse our half-hearted devotion to God. Isn't that so? Let's stop with the games and do what David did: stand in the light of God!

Lord, scrutinize my heart! Show me what is grievous to You, and help me to grow away from it! Amen.

174

Read the road signs

Teach me to do Your will, for You are my God!
Let Your good Spirit lead me on level ground!
PSALM 143:10

How wonderful when life's journey is easy. The best times of our lives are shared with loved ones, working hard and dreaming big. Other times, though, the road can become narrower, steeper, strewn with obstacles.

Then we become very dependent on the guidance of the Holy Spirit, as David prays for here. The guidance of the Spirit is like the road signs along your way. It tells you where you're heading, what to look out for, and where to turn. To merely know the meaning of the different signs is not enough. To make use of them on the journey, at confusing crossroads or where the dangers lie, *that* is helpful!

In the same way, it's not good enough to have a Bible that gathers dust on the shelf, but to use it as you journey along. Then you'll experience the guidance of the Holy Spirit!

Show me the way, Lord.
Lead me, Holy Spirit! Amen.

175

Teach me to fight

> Blessed be the LORD, my rock, who trains
> my hands for war, and my fingers for battle.
> PSALM 144:1

In this verse we are presented with the important fact that life has its conflict and strife. Yes, unfortunately this is the case. We may have thought that since we're serving God our lives should be all peace and harmony, but that is not the case at all! While we're in the world, we'll definitely deal with its brokenness and sinfulness; therefore, we will experience tension, competition, hostility, and struggle!

Yes, as Christians we do need to fight from time to time – for the truth, for what's right, and for those who cannot fight for themselves. We must be able to confront what's wrong and not shy away. Still, we need to learn how to fight correctly, fittingly – as children of God.

We must fight our fights with fairness, honesty, empathy, and kindness. God taught David to stand for what was right. He must teach us as well!

*Lord, empower me to confront the challenges in my life.
Teach me how to do it in Your way. Amen.*

The greatest kingdom ever

Your kingdom is an everlasting kingdom,
and Your dominion endures throughout all generations.

PSALM 145:13

God is king forever, king over all kings! In the New Testament the epithet "King of kings and Lord of lords" is ascribed to Jesus Christ (1 Tim. 6:15). It's a proven fact that Christ, once mockingly called the "king of the Jews" (Luke 23:36-37), is now the greatest king of all time. It's true! Which king has had a reign of two thousand years?

Which king's kingdom is spread out over the whole world? Which king has had as many subjects as our King? Through the ages millions and millions have subjected themselves to Christ! Which king's coming has divided history so radically that new dates and calendars had to be devised?

For which king were so many prepared to change their behavior, their work, their relationships, their plans – or literally give up their lives to die? Well, for King Jesus! Our king is King over all kings – and that is a fact.

Lord, Your kingdom is indeed an everlasting kingdom – Your dominion is forever! Amen.

177

Forget about princes

Put not your trust in princes, in a son of man,
in whom there is no salvation. When his breath departs,
he returns to the earth; on that very day his plans perish.

PSALM 146:3-4

These verses are about the fact that we so easily depend on "princes." We so readily put people on pedestals as role models or even potential benefactors. Of course it's not wrong to look up to people or to depend on someone, but these verses are about trusting people with a trust that no man is worthy of.

These people can perhaps do some things for us, but they will always remain human – and therefore fallible. They cannot save us. Even our significant other can only deliver what he or she can deliver and nothing more.

It's unfair to expect that they fulfill all our needs or save us. No, there is only one Savior, and that is Christ Jesus. Only He can be trusted with our happiness, future, prosperity, and salvation. People will disappoint us, but God never disappoints!

Lord, I trust You with my life! Amen.

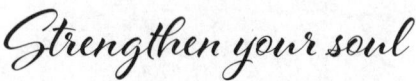

Strengthen your soul

> The LORD builds up Jerusalem; He gathers
> the outcasts of Israel. He heals the
> brokenhearted and binds up their wounds.
>
> PSALM 147:2-3

What is God doing in these verses? Look at the verbs: He builds up, He gathers, He heals, and He binds up. Isn't it beautiful? Yes, God is in the business of restoration and healing – it's His specialty! Are your walls down? Does the enemy run in and out of your soul with little resistance? Do you feel tired or broken down?

Go, then, to God! Take some rest; catch your breath! Let God heal your heart and strengthen your soul again. You will be restored and rejuvenated, your strength renewed, and your thoughts refocused.

You'll be ready to face the world again! Yes, go the heavenly Healer, go with your confusion or tears or frustrations or questions – just go! You so need it! To go to God is never, ever in vain – you'll see!

Lord, I'm coming to You. Heal my heart! Amen.

What matters?

> His delight is not in the strength of the horse,
> nor His pleasure in the legs of a man,
> but the L ORD takes pleasure in those who
> fear Him, in those who hope in His steadfast love.
>
> PSALM 147:10-11

The question that the psalmist is trying to answer is: What is important to God? Is it to be attractive, athletically built, fit, or perhaps popular? Is it important to God that you're well off? Is it important that you have a certain standing in the community?

Let's emphasize that if you enjoy these things you are blessed indeed – praise God! But the question remains: What is important to God? For God, it's important that we are humble, that we can love, that we're grateful for His grace, that we serve Him and trust in Him for this life and the next!

In such a context wealth becomes irrelevant – as does appearance, popularity, or career. Do you serve the Lord? That is the question!

> Lord, I do want to serve You.
> Be the Lord of my life! Amen.

Praise for new reasons

> Praise the Lord! Sing to the Lord a new song,
> His praise in the assembly of the godly!
>
> PSALM 149:1

We are often prompted in the Psalms to sing a "new song" to the Lord. Does this mean that God is bored with the old ones? Fortunately not! God first pays attention to the heart of the worshipper, not so much to the words of his song.

It pleases God that we sing to Him, whether or not we get the words right. We can worship God with any song as long as we have a heart of worship. So, what is a new song? A new song is the result of a heart that is inspired anew, excited anew about God's greatness, finding new reasons for praising God, using new words.

Creative and Spirit-filled artists come up all the time with beautiful new songs, because God is all the time doing new things! Sing a new song – or sing the beautiful old ones for new reasons!

Lord, I do praise and worship You –
in the old and in the new ways! Amen.